The Pasta Salad Book

The Pasta Salad Book

Nina Graybill and Maxine Rapoport

Farragut Publishing Company
Washington, D.C.
1984

Fourth Printing 1986
PRINTED IN THE UNITED STATES OF AMERICA

Book design by Kevin Osborn

Cover illustration by Judy Barczak

Library of Congress Catalog Card Number: 84-81333
ISBN: 0-918535-00-X

For Barry,
who has always wanted to have a book
dedicated to him
N.G.

To Dan,
for his
encouragement
M.R.

Introduction

*P*asta salads--delicious, colorful and unusual. An added bonus is that they're simple to prepare, yet look sophisticated. Pasta salads can be made well in advance of serving, rely on fresh and nutritious ingredients, and contain hints of cultures and cuisines from around the world. While some pasta salads seem best suited as refreshing summertime dishes—especially when certain vegetables and herbs are at their peak—others qualify as winter favorites, satisfying the heartiest of eaters with full-bodied flavors. Most, however, are suited for serving all year round. Some pasta salads taste best chilled, others at room temperature or warm.

Pasta salads are remarkably adaptable. They can cost a few pennies a serving or call for a real splurge. They can be served as first courses, entrees or side dishes. What's more, they are as suitable for an elegant dinner party or buffet as they are for the family table.

As with any type of salad, quality and freshness count. Use pasta made from semolina or durum wheat flour—it holds its shape and texture. And if you make your own pasta, it would be worth your while to search out this type of flour, at least for pasta salads. Invest in a bottle of extra-virgin olive oil. Use whatever type of salad oil you prefer, as long as it is fresh smelling and tasting. A bottle of good wine vinegar doesn't cost that much but adds an extra fillip to dressings. Don't shy away from recipes that call for sesame paste, sesame oil or Chinese hot oil—these ingredients are found in the import sections of most large supermarkets, will last indefinitely if refrigerated and can be used in a variety of other dishes as well.

A word on substitutions: Feel free to use one vegetable in place of another, but keep in mind that the character of the dish may change— especially when only one or two vegetables are used. With pasta, the important thing is keeping the shapes similar—any long, thin pasta can be used in recipes calling for linguine, for example, just as shells could be substituted for, say, wagonwheel pasta.

Some other tips:

Cook pasta only until al dente—meaning cooked through but still firm to the bite. Start testing packaged pasta after 5 minutes or so. The instant the pasta reaches the al dente stage, quickly drain it. Most fresh pasta cooks in mere minutes.

If the pasta is to be mixed with a dressing or sauce well in advance of serving, reserve a little sauce. Since pasta tends to absorb liquid, you may want to add a little more dressing just before serving.

Chilling tends to decrease the intensity of some flavors and the recipes in this book take this effect into account. You may still want to taste a chilled salad just before serving and adjust seasonings to your own taste.

Presentation is important too. Clear salad bowls show off layered salads. Pasta salads heaped on serving platters invite attractive garnishes. Soup tureens, baskets lined with foil, trays and casseroles all make attractive serving pieces for pasta salads.

These recipes serve six.

We have assembled more than 150 recipes for this book. Some are our own creations, others were passed on by friends, still others have been adapted from restaurant favorites, gourmet carry-out delicacies and various publications. We would like to thank the contributors, known and unknown, who have given us so many hours of pleasurable testing and tasting. We hope you enjoy our pasta salad recipes as well.

Nina Graybill and Maxine Rapoport

Contents

Pasta Salads with Vegetables   1

Pasta Capri   4
Fresh tomatoes, peppers, mozzarella and basil tossed with warm penne

Low-Calorie Hot Spaghetti with Cold Vegetable Sauce   5
Spaghetti, tomatoes and cucumbers in a spicy sauce

Spaghetti with Fresh Tomatoes and Mozzarella   6
Hot spaghetti with fresh mozzarella, tomatoes and basil

Angel Hair with Tomato and Basil Sauce   7
Capellini with fresh tomatoes, basil and capers

Gnocchi with Tart Tomato Sauce   8
Jumbo tomato pasta shells, lemon and garlic-marinated tomatoes with fresh basil and parsley

Spaghetti and Mozzarella Salad   9
Warm spaghetti and cheese with tomatoes, snow peas and green peas

Vermicelli in Tomato Shells   10
Summer-ripe tomatoes stuffed with vermicelli and pesto sauce

Onions Oriental and Vermicelli   11
Vermicelli tossed with small white onions, a spicy curried dressing, pine nuts and white raisins

Oriental Primavera and Vermicelli   12
Green beans, cauliflower, zucchini and radishes tossed with vermicelli and a spicy sesame-soy dressing

Fettuccine and Feta   13
Fettuccine, feta cheese, fresh or frozen snow peas, Greek olives, peppers and cherry tomatoes bathed with a red wine dressing

Spinach and Rotelle Salad   14
Fresh spinach stir-fried with anchovies, garlic, parsley and pine nuts, then mixed with rotelle

Cold Vegetable and Rotini Salad   15
Rotini layered with broccoli, snow peas, green beans, carrots, cherry tomatoes and walnuts

Caesar's Pasta 16
Vermicelli, romaine lettuce and croutons with a classic Caesar dressing

Twists and Eggplant 17
Diced eggplant, tomatoes, celery, onions, garlic and herbs mixed with twist pasta

Eggplant and Linguine Salad 18
Linguine, sauteed eggplant, capers and garlic-flavored olive oil

✳ Vegetables Vinaigrette with Rotelle 19
Marinated cauliflower, broccoli, carrots, green beans with rotelle in a vinaigrette dressing

Winter Pasta Salad 20
Broccoli, jarred Italian vegetables, pimiento and twist pasta with a creamy dressing

A Pasta Salad with Character 21
Penne or elbow macaroni, cherry tomatoes, cured black olives, red onion and parsley in a hearty dressing that includes pepper flakes, capers and anchovies

Pickled Shells 22
Pasta mixed with dill pickles and a sour cream dressing

✳ Low Salt, Low Fat Cold Pasta Salad (with Variations) 23
Rotini or shells with tomatoes, cucumber, red onion, peppers, potatoes, broccoli and green beans with an apple juice dressing

White Kidney Bean and Macaroni Salad Bibb 24
White beans, sweet pepper, parsley, cherry tomatoes and macaroni tossed with oil and vinegar

Pasta Salad Nicoise 25
Layers of short pasta, eggs, tomatoes, anchovies, capers and pimiento dressed with a garlicky sauce

Tomatoes Nicoise and Linguine 26
Marinated tomatoes and black olives with linguine, parsley and Parmesan cheese

Fettuccine and Tomatoes in Lemon Sauce 27
Fettuccine in lemon dressing mixed with fresh tomatoes and basil leaves

Garden-Fresh Pasta Salad 28
Tube pasta with green beans, green and yellow squash, eggplant, green pepper and pesto sauce

Vegetable and Pasta Salad with Pizazz 29
Fettuccine, broccoli and cherry tomatoes tossed with a red pepper dressing

Roasted Pepper, Zucchini and Pasta Salad 30
Rotelle or penne, zucchini and roasted red peppers with a garlic and oregano dressing

Artichoke and Pasta Salad with Tomato Sauce 31
Ziti, artichokes and tomatoes with herb dressing

Fettuccine and Mushroom Salad 32
Fresh mushrooms and green onions marinated in a creamy sauce, then
tossed with chilled pasta

Broccoli, Walnut Primavera 33
Fettuccine, broccoli, tomatoes, black olives and walnuts in a vinegar-flavored
pesto sauce

Pasta Primavera, Again 34
Ribbon pasta with steamed zucchini, broccoli, green beans and herbs

Crunchy and Creamy Curried Pasta Salad 35
Short-shaped pasta, green pepper, celery, green onions, pimiento in a creamy
curried dressing

Ultra-Simple Green Pasta Salad 36
Green fettuccine, pimientos, green onions and sunflower seeds tossed with
a creamy dressing

Linguine Salad Foster 37
Linguine tossed with sliced cured black olives, anchovies and parsley

Sweet and Sour Orzo and Vegetable Salad 38
Orzo pasta and chopped cucumbers, carrots, green onions in a sweet-sour
dressing

Mystery Garden Pasta Salad 39
Linguine, broccoli, carrots, cherry tomatoes, green onions, with a wheat
germ and sesame flavored dressing

Sesame Pasta Salad 40
Linguine and watercress with spicy sesame-soy dressing

Szechuan Dan Dan Noodles 41
Vermicelli in a ginger-flavored soy dressing

Sutton Place Gourmet Oriental Pasta Salad 42
Whole wheat fusilli, sesame oil and soy sauce mixed with green onions, baby
corn, bamboo shoots, water chestnuts, shredded carrots and cubed tofu

Ginger and Scallion Lo Mein Salad 43
Thin egg noodles, scallions and fresh ginger with chicken broth and soy
sauce

Simple Oriental Noodle Salad 44
Rice sticks or capellini tossed with olive, sesame and sesame-chili oils,
vinegar, toasted sesame seeds, chives and parsley

Fettuccine in Walnut Sauce 45
Fettuccine in parsley, walnut and garlic sauce

San Remo Pasta Salad, Fete Accomplie 46

Sun-dried tomatoes, fresh basil, grated Parmesan cheese, black olives and fusilli with a mild oil and vinegar flavored dressing

Tortellini Salad 47

Tortellini, red peppers (or pimientos), green onions, black olives and walnuts in a dilled vinaigrette

Agnolotti and Tomato Salad 48

Agnolotti or tortellini, tomatoes, mozzarella and Italian olives with a basil vinegar and oil dressing

Rotelle, Mushrooms and Broccoli with a Creamy Tomato Sauce 49

Rotelle and crisp broccoli with a sauce of sauteed fresh mushrooms, light cream, tomatoes and herbs

Shells, Peas and Banana Peppers 50

Fresh peas, long sweet yellow peppers and fontina cheese, mixed with shell pasta, basil flavored oil and vinegar dressing

Linguine with Artichoke, Basil and Walnut Sauce 51

Spinach linguine, frozen artichoke hearts, garlic and walnuts sauteed in olive oil and mixed with fresh basil, parsley and oregano

Not Low-Cal Pasta, Mushroom and Pepper Salad 52

Spinach tagliatelle, fresh mushrooms marinated in lemon juice, green and red peppers in a creamy dressing of mayonnaise, creme fraiche, lemon juice and herbs

Capellini with Broccoli and Goat Cheese 53

Capellini or vermicelli tossed with sauteed broccoli florets, thyme and garlic, and slivers of goat cheese

Vegetarian Pasta Salad La Prima 54

Blanched green beans, zucchini, sweet pickles, Bermuda onion, capers, black olives and rotelle or rotini with a creamy dressing

Mostaciolli and Broccoli with Creamy Garlic Sauce 55

Blanched fresh broccoli and mostaciolli mixed with a sour cream, mayonnaise, garlic and tarragon flavored sauce

Marinated Vegetables with Unadorned Pasta 56

Carrots, zucchini, cauliflower, green pepper, green onions, radishes and cherry tomatoes marinated in a low-calorie dressing and served with plain rotelle

Healthful Vegetable and Orzo Salad 57

Tiny pasta tossed with chopped peppers, radishes, cucumber, parsley and a curried yogurt sauce

Almost Classic Pasta Salad 58

Shell pasta marinated in lemon juice and olive oil, then mixed with green onions, celery, parsley, pimiento olives, green pepper, hard-cooked eggs, sunflower seeds and a mayonnaise and sour cream dressing

Pasta Salad Bar — 59

Pasta of your choice with suggested accompaniments

Pasta Salads with Poultry — 61

Indonesian Spaghetti and Chicken — 64

Ramen noodles (or thin spaghetti), chicken, peas, radishes and cucumbers in a spicy peanut butter and soy sauce

Cold Chicken and Noodles in a Spicy Sesame Sauce — 65

Linguine and poached chicken with sesame, soy and wine vinegar dressing

Chinese Noodle and Chicken Salad with Peanut Sauce — 66

Thin noodles and chicken garnished with bean sprouts, carrots, cucumbers, green onions and baby corn on the cob with a gingered soy peanut sauce

Chinese Noodle and Mushroom Salad with Chicken and Ham — 67

Fine egg noodles, black Chinese mushrooms, chicken, ham, water chestnuts, green onions and cilantro (or parsley) combined with a chili and sesame oil dressing

Stir-Fried Chicken, Linguine and Peanuts — 68

Linguine, chicken, green peppers, carrots and scallions stir-fried with broth, soy and sherry

Hacked Chicken and Noodles in a Spicy Sauce — 69

Vermicelli, chicken and cucumbers and sauce seasoned with Szechuan peppercorns, ginger and sesame seed paste

Oriental Chicken and Pasta with Fruit — 70

Twist pasta, poached and shredded chicken, pineapple, grapes, celery and water chestnuts and a light tarragon, soy dressing

Sesame Chicken and Twists Salad — 71

Pasta twists, chicken, snow peas, water chestnuts and scallions with sesame seeds and a mustard and sherry sauce

Fettuccine and Chicken Nicoise Salad — 72

Chicken breast, tomatoes, capers, fresh dill, and mayonnaise tossed with fettuccine

Chicken, Green Pepper and Linguine, Oriental Style — 73

Linguine, chicken, green peppers, scallions, dried hot peppers and Szechuan peppercorns in a soy dressing

Chicken and Noodles in a Chinese Chili Paste Sauce — 74

Thin spaghetti and chicken with sauteed scallions and a sauce flavored with cold tea and chili paste

Layered Chicken and Pasta Salad — 75

Macaroni, curry-flavored chicken layered with lettuce, cucumber, green pepper and green onions with a lemon and mayonnaise dressing

Dilled Chicken and Linguine Salad 76

Linguine, chicken, dill pickles, celery, green onions, capers, pimientos and cooked eggs with a creamy dill dressing

Green Noodles with Prosciutto and Chicken 77

Green linguine, chicken, prosciutto, tomatoes, green onions, mushrooms and parsley in a creamy dressing

Rotelle and Chicken Salad 78

Rotelle, left-over chicken, broccoli, sweet pepper, cherry tomatoes, mushrooms and almonds

Chicken and Snow Peas with Fruit and Pasta 79

Spaghetti, chicken, nectarines, red plums, snow peas, green onions and walnuts with a rosemary-flavored vinaigrette

Hot Chicken and Pasta Salad 80

Twist pasta, chicken, cherry tomatoes, water chestnuts, mushrooms, scallions and celery with soy sauce

Vermicelli and Chicken Salad with Lemon Dressing 81

Vermicelli, chicken, bean sprouts, bamboo shoots with lemon and chicken broth sauce

Orzo and Poultry Salad 82

Orzo, left-over chicken or turkey, green onions, celery and parsley with creamy tarragon dressing

Creamy and Curried Chicken, Apple and Fusilli Salad 83

Curried mayonnaise mixed with fusilli or fettuccine, chicken, apples, celery, ripe olives, green onions, almonds and raisins

Mostaccioli, Turkey and Vegetable Salad 84

Mostaccioli, left-over turkey, peas, green beans, radishes and scallions in vinaigrette

Turkey with Ginger and Linguine 85

Linguine, turkey, green onions, peas, almonds, red sweet pepper or pimiento and a ginger and mustard dressing

Turkey and Asparagus Pasta Salad 86

Bow tie or farfalle pasta, turkey, fresh asparagus, tomatoes and watercress tossed with a creamy ricotta cheese sauce

Main Course Pasta "Club" Salad 87

Cubed turkey, bacon, tomatoes, iceberg lettuce and Swiss cheese tossed with rotini and a mayonnaise-based dressing

Turkey Tetrazzini Salad Norwood 88

Linguine, turkey, mushrooms, peas, pimientos and almonds mixed with a spicy cottage cheese dressing

Pepperoni and Shell Salad Bloch 92

Shell pasta, pepperoni, artichoke hearts, sweet peppers, broccoli and pimientos with a creamy basil dressing

Pasta Deli Salad 93

Twist or shell pasta, salami, provolone cheese, red onion, sweet peppers, olives and parsley in a mustard vinaigrette dressing

Antipasto Salad Platter 94

Shell pasta, sweet peppers, mushrooms, provolone cheese, chick peas, salami, Greek olives and anchovies

Colorful Vegetables and Pasta with Pancetta 95

Dried gnocchi or cavatelli and blanched broccoli tossed with cauliflower, mushrooms, green onions and ripe olives marinated in herbed vinaigrette dressing, pancetta, avocado, tomatoes and additional herb dressing

Salami, Garbanzo Beans and Penne a la Tuscany 96

Penne, hard salami, garbanzo beans, red onion, capers, parsley and ripe olives tossed with a garlicky wine vinegar dressing

Rotelle, Ham and Fontina Cheese Salad Lewis 97

Rotelle, ham, red cabbage, fontina or Swiss cheese and walnuts with a mustard dressing

Vermicelli with Asparagus and Ham 98

Vermicelli and ham with stir-fried fresh asparagus and onions

Pasta and Ham Layered Salad 99

Macaroni, lettuce, ham, cooked eggs, peas, Monterey Jack cheese and a creamy dressing

Pasta and Ham Picnic Salad 100

Rigatoni or elbow pasta, ham, sweet peppers, red onion, sweet pickles, cherry tomatoes, cooked eggs and fresh dill mixed with a tart dressing

Rotelle with Beef and Mushrooms 101

Rotelle or twist pasta, grilled flank steak, mushrooms, dill pickles, tomatoes and cooked eggs in a caper- and tarragon-flavored dressing

Beef, Snow Peas, Mushrooms with Bow Tie Pasta and Bleu Cheese Dressing 102

Bow tie or farfalle pasta, rare roast beef, mushrooms, snow peas and watercress in a bleu cheese dressing

Piquant Beef, Cherry Tomato and Pasta Salad 103

Rotelle or shell pasta, roast beef, cherry tomatoes, green onions, parsley, capers, fresh basil and cured black olives in an anchovy-flavored dressing

Beef and Pasta with Broccoli and Asparagus 104

Fettuccine, flank steak, broccoli and fresh asparagus with a gingered
soy dressing

Corned Beef, Crunchy Cabbage and Pasta 105

Twist pasta, corned beef, cabbage, carrots, celery, green pepper and green
onions mixed with creamy garlic dressing

Rotelle with Cabbage and Beef 106

Rotelle, cabbage, left-over pot roast and caraway seeds with red wine
vinegar dressing

Lamb, Green Bean and Orzo Salad 107

Orzo or tiny pasta, cooked lamb, green beans, red onion, sweet pepper and
and parsley tossed with a mustard and rosemary vinaigrette dressing

Lamb or Beef with Wheels or Shells 108

Pasta, cooked lamb or beef, onion, parsley, sweet peppers, celery,
cucumbers, tomatoes and black olives in a herb and caper dressing

Italian Sausage and Vegetables with Wheels 109

Wheel or elbow pasta, mild Italian sausage, zucchini, green pepper, pimiento,
Italian cured black olives with oil and vinegar

Shells, Sausage and Peppers 110

Shell pasta, sweet and hot Italian sausage, green peppers, garlic, parsley
and white wine

Spaghetti, Italian Sausages and Red Peppers in a Sprightly Sauce 111

Spaghetti and sauteed sausage mixed with a sauce of chili-flavored
oil, canned plum tomatoes, sweet red peppers and herbs

Primavera with Italian Sausage 112

Twist pasta, sweet and hot Italian sausage, fresh asparagus, mushrooms,
cherry tomatoes and parsley tossed with a simple oil and vinegar dressing

Pasta Salad Todi 113

Sun-dried tomatoes, red and green peppers, cherry tomatoes, Genoa and
cervalat salami, Parmesan cheese and fresh basil combined with rigatoni
and a mustard-based vinaigrette dressing

Fusilli Salad with Bacon and Cheese 114

Fusilli, Parmesan cheese, crisp bacon and fresh herbs lightly tossed with a
raspberry vinegar flavored vinaigrette dressing

Pasta Salads with Seafood 115

Pasta and Tuna Suzanne 119

Short type pasta, tuna, red pepper, broccoli, Parmesan cheese and fresh
basil mixed with a mayonnaise and tomato sauce dressing

Tuna, Broccoli and Red Peppers with Farfalle 120

Farfalle or bow tie pasta, broccoli, red sweet peppers, tuna, Italian olives tossed with capers and oregano-seasoned dressing

Pasta Salad with Tuna and Greek Olives 121

Rigatoni or short pasta, tuna, black Greek olives, and cherry tomatoes with lemon juice, oil and capers

Tuscany Tuna, Bean and Pasta Salad 122

Shell pasta, white beans, tuna, red onion and parsley in a sage-flavored vinaigrette dressing

Tuna, Pasta and White Bean Salad 123

Penne or ziti, tuna, white beans, cornichons or dill pickles, capers, mild fresh peppers and spinach with a lemon-flavored creamy dressing

Rotelle and Tuna with Broccoli 124

Rotelle, tuna, broccoli, sweet red pepper, watercress and red onion in vinaigrette with red pepper flakes

Tuna and Carrot Pasta Salad 125

Short pasta, tuna, carrots, celery, green onions, dill pickles and hard-cooked eggs in a creamy garlic sauce

Pasta Salad with Tuna 126

Fettuccine, pine nuts, tomatoes, tuna, sweet red pepper, black olives, parsley with olive oil and red wine vinegar

Tuna and Garden Delight Farfalle Salad 127

Farfalle, tuna, broccoli, zucchini, mushrooms, tomatoes and red onion

Tart Tuna and Orzo Salad 128

Orzo, tuna, red onion, tomato and parsley mixed with a lemon and tarragon vinegar dressing

Salmon and Pasta with Carrots and Watercress 129

Wheel or shell pasta, fresh or canned salmon, carrots, watercress, Italian olives and capers with a mustard and tarragon vinaigrette

Summer Salmon and Shells 130

Shell pasta, iceberg lettuce, ripe olives, cherry tomatoes, cucumbers and canned salmon in dill mayonnaise

Any Season Salmon and Shell Salad 131

Shell or elbow pasta, canned salmon, carrots, celery, pimiento-stuffed olives, peas, parsley, onion and sweet pepper with a tart vinaigrette dressing

Fish and Thin Noodles, Oriental Style 132

Spaghettini or Chinese egg noodles, fish fillets, bean sprouts, carrot, green onion tops tossed in an Oriental peanut butter sauce

Seaside Spaghetti 133

Spaghettini or linguine, fish fillets, shrimp, tomatoes, and onions in a white wine sauce

Seafood, Pasta and Vegetable Salad 134

Mostaccioli, flounder fillets, shrimp, scallions, zucchini, leeks and peas in a creamy cucumber dressing

Delicate Oriental Noodle and Seafood Salad 135

Cellophane noodles or vermicelli, shrimp, scallops, celery, watercress, pimiento and cucumber with a hot green onion, lemon and soy sauce

Rice Noodles and Shrimp with Vegetables 136

Rice noodles, shrimp, fresh spinach, mushrooms, green onions, zucchini and radishes in a soy dressing with five-spice powder

Herb-Dressed Shrimp and Pasta Salad 137

Twist or shell pasta, shrimp and parsley with a lemon and herb dressing

Shrimp, Ham and Penne with Dilled Vinaigrette 138

Penne or rotini, shrimp, ham steak, cooked eggs, red onion, cucumber, ripe olives and pimiento tossed with a fresh dill vinaigrette

Low-Calorie Linguine with Shrimp-Yogurt Sauce 139

Linguine, shrimp, parsley and scallions mixed with yogurt, lemon zest and herbs

Orzo and Shrimp Salad 140

Orzo or tiny pasta, shrimp, parsley and capers with a creamy dill sauce

Pasta- and Shrimp-Stuffed Tomato Shells 141

Orzo or tiny pasta, tomatoes, shrimp, cucumber, green pepper, green onions and a dill vinaigrette dressing

Jumbo Shells Stuffed with Crabmeat 142

Jumbo shells, crabmeat, capers, pine nuts and parsley with vinaigrette dressing

Herbed Scallops and Linguine 143

Linguine and scallops mixed with capers and mayonnaise dressing

Fettuccine with Scallops and Langostinos 144

Scallops marinated in fresh lime juice then mixed with langostinos or shrimp and fettuccine

Scallop, Green Bean and Wagonwheel Salad 145

Wheel or shell pasta, scallops, green beans, scallions and red lettuce with fresh dill dressing

Curried Mussel Salad with Tiny Pasta 146

Pasta, mussels, frozen peas, celery leaves or parsley, mixed with two curried dressings

Mussels Marinara with Linguine 147

Linguine and mussels with lemon-sparked marinara sauce

Fettuccine and Mussel Salad 148

Fettuccine, mussels, onion, celery, green onions and garlic in a creamy wine sauce

Mussels and Pasta in Sauce Verte   149

Shell pasta tossed with Basic Vinaigrette and mussels topped with Sauce Verte

Shell Pasta with Mussels and Broccoli   150

Shells, mussels and mushrooms with a mustard dressing

Shells with Shrimp, Scallops and Snow Peas   151

Shells, shrimp, scallops, snow peas, cucumbers and celery with a mustard, sesame and soy dressing

Linguine and Mixed Seafood Salad   152

Linguine, squid, mussels and clams mixed with lemon and oil and garnished with red onion and parsley

Fusilli and Mussels in Spinach Sauce   153

Mussels cooked in a ginger-flavored wine and lemon juice broth, then mixed with fusilli and a creamy spinach, parsley and ginger sauce

Shells and Swedish Herring Salad   154

Shell pasta, pickled herring, diced boiled potatoes, cooked beets, apples, onions, dill, cucumber and mayonnaise mixed and chilled several hours

Chilled Squid Salad with Spaghettini   155

Squid marinated in lemon juice, olive oil and herbs, then tossed with spaghettini

Salad Dressings and Sauces   157

Basic Vinaigrette   160

Olive oil or half olive and half salad, vinegar, dry mustard, salt and pepper

Herbed Vinaigrette   161

Olive oil, white wine vinegar, mustard and herbs

Dill Vinaigrette   162

Oil, white wine vinegar, mustard and fresh dill

Sesame Seed Vinaigrette   163

Oil, wine vinegar, garlic and sauteed sesame seeds

Tarragon and Soy Vinaigrette   164

Olive oil, tarragon vinegar, soy sauce, fresh or dried tarragon and sesame oil

Anchovy Dressing   165

Anchovy fillets, wine vinegar, mustard and oil

Sauce Verte   166

Mayonnaise, spinach, parsley, watercress, chives, dill, tarragon and lemon juice

Herb Sauce   167

Olive oil blended with watercress, parsley, green onions and mustard

Creamy Garlic Sauce 168

Sour cream, mayonnaise, tarragon or wine vinegar, olive oil, tarragon and garlic

Parsley Pesto 169

Parsley, walnuts, Parmesan cheese, garlic and olive oil

Spinach Pesto 170

Frozen spinach, parsley, Parmesan cheese, pine nuts or walnuts, garlic and olive oil

Spinach and Parsley Pesto 171

Fresh spinach, parsley, olive oil, Parmesan or Romano cheese, pine nuts, oregano and garlic

Creamy Pesto Sauce 172

Fresh basil, hard-cooked eggs, oil, garlic, basil or white wine vinegar and Parmesan cheese

Low-Calorie Creamy Dressing 173

Mayonnaise, low-fat yogurt, tarragon, mustard and dried herbs

Low-Calorie Mustard Vinaigrette 174

Dijon mustard, apple juice concentrate, lemon juice and dried herbs

Pasta Salads
with Vegetables

Pasta Salads with Vegetables

*D*on't pass this section by just because it's the middle of winter. While a number of these pasta salads do require the fresh vegetables of spring and summer, many more use vegetables that are available year round. If there are vegetarians in your family, vegetable pasta salads are a nutritious and tasty alternative to tofu and brown rice.

Colors and textures are especially important in vegetable pasta salads. When cooked vegetables are called for, barely blanch them and immediately rinse them under cold water to stop the cooking and to set the color. Both vinegar and lemon juice will, over time, turn green vegetables an olive color. Therefore, you may want to mix dressings and green vegetables shortly before serving; simply toss the pasta with part of the dressing beforehand so it can absorb the flavor and reserve the rest for a last-minute mixing with the vegetables.

Pasta Capri

A real crowd pleaser. A "do-ahead" warm weather menu could include cold poached chicken breasts napped with tarragon mayonnaise, toasted pita bread with lemon butter and for dessert, cold pear halves poached in raspberry vinegar syrup and crisp shortbread wedges.

8 ounces penne or small rigatoni

5 large tomatoes

4 cloves garlic, minced

25 leaves of fresh basil, torn into large pieces

3 long sweet yellow peppers or 2 sweet green peppers

8 ounces mozzarella cheese, cubed

Freshly grated Parmesan cheese

Dressing

1/2 cup olive oil

1-1/2 teaspoons salt

1/2 teaspoon freshly ground pepper

At least 2 hours before serving, slice the tomatoes, then slice again into strips. Seed peppers and cut into thin rounds if using yellow peppers or into thin strips if using green peppers.

In a small bowl mix the tomatoes, peppers, garlic, basil leaves, oil, salt and pepper. Let stand without refrigerating.

Just before serving, cook pasta until al dente, drain well and put into a large shallow bowl. Add the mozzarella and the tomato mixture, toss and serve immediately. Pass grated Parmesan at the table.

Serves 6.

Low-Calorie Hot Spaghetti with Cold Vegetable Sauce

A simple and quickly made salad that is also low in calories. This side dish is especially good with grilled chicken or meat.

12 ounces spaghetti or linguine

3 cups coarsely chopped fresh tomatoes
(or canned plum tomatoes, well drained)

1-1/2 cups peeled and seeded cucumber, cubed

2 cloves garlic, quartered

1/4 teaspoon oregano

1/2 teaspoon basil

Salt and pepper to taste

Tabasco sauce, if desired, to taste
(about 1/2 teaspoon)

Cook pasta until al dente, drain well.

While pasta is cooking, whirl rest of ingredients, including Tabasco if desired, in food processor or blender until almost smooth—leaving some of the vegetables in tiny pieces. Taste, adjust seasonings.

Toss sauce with hot spaghetti and serve.

Serves 6.

Spaghetti with Fresh Tomatoes and Mozzarella

*T*he secret to this salad is fresh mozzarella, available at Italian delis and gourmet shops. If you must use packaged mozzarella, make it the whole milk variety.

1 pound spaghetti

6 ripe tomatoes, cut into small cubes

8 ounces fresh mozzarella, cut into small cubes

20 fresh basil leaves, torn into quarters

1 cup olive oil, or to taste

Salt and pepper to taste

Cook spaghetti to al dente stage, drain well. Toss while hot with remaining ingredients. Serve while still warm.

Serves 6.

Angel Hair with Tomato and Basil Sauce

Subtle flavor in the sauce lifts a simple pasta dish to "angelic" heights.

12 ounces capellini or angel hair pasta

2 pounds fresh plum tomatoes, not canned

3/4 cup fresh basil leaves, coarsely chopped

3-1/4 ounce jar capers, rinsed and drained

3 tablespoons sherry vinegar or 2 table-spoons vinegar and 1 tablespoon sherry

1/2 teaspoon salt

1/2 teaspoon freshly ground pepper

1/2 cup olive oil

*P*eel, seed and chop tomatoes. (Do not use a food processor.)

*C*ombine with the chopped basil and refrigerate overnight or prepare a few hours before serving but do not refrigerate.

*T*wo hours before serving add the vinegar (or sherry and vinegar combination), capers and salt and pepper. Do not refrigerate.

*J*ust before serving time add pasta to boiling, salted water and cook barely 4 minutes. Drain well and transfer to a rimmed platter or shallow bowl and toss with 1/2 cup olive oil. Add the tomato and basil sauce and serve.

Serves 6.

Gnocchi with Tart Tomato Sauce

*A*nother variation of a cold tomato sauce to make up early before the heat of the summer day sets in.

12 ounces dried gnocchi, conchiglie or cavatelli, tomato flavored if possible though plain will do nicely

2 pounds garden-ripe tomatoes, seeded and roughly chopped

4 cloves garlic, minced

1/4 cup lemon juice

Grated rind of lemon

1-1/2 teaspoons salt

1/2 teaspoon freshly ground black pepper

1/2 cup olive oil

1/4 cup basil vinegar

1/2 teaspoon sugar

1/4 cup finely chopped basil leaves

1/4 cup finely chopped parsley

Freshly grated Parmesan cheese

*I*n a large serving bowl marinate chopped tomatoes, garlic, lemon juice and rind, salt, pepper, olive oil, vinegar and sugar. This mixture can marinate any number of hours, but do not refrigerate.

*A*bout 1 hour before serving cook pasta until al dente, drain, rinse with cold water and drain again. Toss with 1 tablespoon olive oil.

*A*dd the chopped basil and parsley to the tomato marinade.

*A*t serving time add the pasta to the tomato mixture and toss to coat the pasta.

*P*ass the Parmesan cheese separately.

*S*erves 6.

Spaghetti and Mozzarella Salad

*P*asta with a creamy texture and a tangy taste. This is a nice side dish with any broiled or sauteed meat.

12 ounces spaghetti or fusilli

1 tablespoon olive oil

8 ounces mozzarella cheese, shredded

3 tomatoes, chopped

1/2 cup watercress, chopped

1/2 pound fresh snow peas, blanched, or one box frozen snow peas, thawed only

1/2 box frozen tiny green peas, thawed only

2 garlic cloves, minced

1 teaspoon salt

1/2 teaspoon freshly ground pepper

1/2 cup grated Parmesan cheese

Dressing

1/3 cup olive oil

3 tablespoons herb vinegar

1/2 teaspoon sugar

*C*ook spaghetti to al dente stage, drain well, and toss with 1 tablespoon olive oil.

*A*dd the shredded cheese to the hot pasta and stir over very low heat until cheese melts. (Don't worry if cheese seems gummy—it will separate when the other ingredients are added.) Remove from heat and toss gently with the remaining ingredients. Add dressing and toss again.

*S*erve at room temperature. Pass the Parmesan separately.

*S*erves 6.

Vermicelli in Tomato Shells

A *perfect first course in the summer when tomatoes and basil are at their peak. When tomatoes are out of season, serve the vermicelli by itself. And when fresh basil is lacking, try one of the pesto-type sauces on pages 169-172.*

1/2 pound of vermicelli

6 ripe tomatoes

1/2 cup pesto sauce (recipe below)

4 ounces pine nuts (or chopped walnuts)

Grated Parmesan cheese

Fresh basil leaves for garnish (optional)

Salt and pepper to taste

Pesto Sauce

2 cups fresh basil leaves

3 cloves garlic

About 1 cup grated Parmesan and Romano cheese, mixed

3/4 cup olive oil

*H*ollow out tomatoes and drain well upside down. (Reserve tomato pulp for a cooked sauce, if desired.)

*C*ook vermicelli to al dente stage and drain well.

*W*hile pasta is cooking, make pesto sauce by whirling sauce ingredients in the blender until smooth.

*T*oss vermicelli and pine nuts with pesto sauce, season to taste with more grated cheese and salt and pepper. Fill tomatoes with pasta and garnish with optional basil leaves.

*S*erves 6.

Onions Oriental and Vermicelli

An unusual side dish or first course that will give your guests a pleasant surprise.

8 ounces vermicelli

2 dozen small white onions—the smaller the better (Try the frozen ones.)

1/4 cup chopped parsley

1/4 cup pine nuts

1/2 teaspoon freshly ground pepper

Dressing

1/4 cup olive oil

2 teaspoons curry powder, or more to taste

1 teaspoon ground coriander

1/2 teaspoon ground cardomom or seeds from 4 cardomom pods

1/4 teaspoon turmeric

2 cloves garlic, minced

1 teaspoon salt

1 cup beef or chicken broth

1/2 cup white raisins

Cook vermicelli until al dente, drain, rinse under cold water and drain again. Transfer to a serving bowl and toss with 1 tablespoon olive oil. Do not refrigerate.

Parboil peeled onions for 5 minutes in boiling, salted water, or slip peels off after boiling. If using frozen onions, simply thaw.

In medium-size saucepan heat the oil, then add curry powder, coriander, cardomom and turmeric. Heat spices for a few minutes until fragrance is released. Add garlic, then parboiled onions, salt and broth. Boil uncovered for about 5 minutes, stirring occasionally. Remove the onions with a slotted spoon and add the raisins to the cooking liquid. Cook for 5 more minutes, then pour liquid over the onions. Add the parsley, pine nuts and ground pepper and let stand at room temperature for a few hours before serving.

At serving time add to the pasta and toss gently.

Serves 6.

Oriental Primavera
and Vermicelli

This salad would be a fitting accompaniment to any number of Oriental main dishes such as crispy soy-marinated chicken, gingered shrimp and scallops on skewers, or beef with chili peppers.

12 ounces vermicelli

1 pound green beans, trimmed and cut in half

2 cups cauliflower, broken into bite-size florets

1 cup thinly sliced zucchini

1/2 cup thinly sliced red radishes

1/4 cup toasted sesame seeds for garnish

Dressing

1/2 cup salad oil

1 tablespoon sesame oil

1/4 cup soy sauce

1/4 cup white wine vinegar

3 tablespoons dry sherry

1 tablespoon sugar

1/2 teaspoon salt

1 tablespoon minced garlic

Cook vermicelli until al dente and drain. Toss with 1 tablespoon salad oil and set aside to cool.

Bring a pot of salted water to the boil. Add cauliflower and blanch 1 minute. Remove with a slotted spoon and rinse under cold water. Drain and set aside to cool. Add beans to the boiling water and blanch for 2 minutes. Remove and rinse under cold water and cool completely.

Heat oil in small frying pan over medium heat. Saute garlic until barely golden. Remove pan from heat and add soy sauce, vinegar, sherry, sugar and salt.

Arrange vermicelli on a serving platter and add cauliflower, beans, zucchini and radishes in an attractive pattern.

Drizzle dressing on top and sprinkle with sesame seeds. Toss at the table before serving.

Serves 6.

Fettuccine and Feta

_____

_____

_____

*T*his salad hints of the Greek Isles and is a fine beginning or side dish for a dinner that includes a leg of lamb roasted with garlic and oregano.

12 ounces fettuccine, fresh if available

1/4 pound feta cheese, cubed or coarsely crumbled

1 box frozen snow peas, thawed only, or 1/4 pound fresh if available

1/4 pound black Greek olives

1 sweet green, red or yellow pepper, cut in strips

1/2 box cherry tomatoes, cut in half if large

1/2 cup chopped walnuts

Dressing

2/3 cup olive oil

4 tablespoons red wine vinegar

salt and pepper to taste

1 teaspoon oregano

1/2 teaspoon dried mint, crushed

*C*ook fettuccine to al dente stage, drain well. Combine with cheese, vegetables and walnuts.

*S*hake olive oil, vinegar, oregano, mint and salt and pepper in small jar until well combined; pour a quarter cup of the dressing at a time over the salad, mixing well after each addition—you may need less than the entire amount. Adjust seasonings. Serve at room temperature.

*S*erves 6.

Spinach and Rotelle Salad

This healthful salad makes a nice substitute for the usual rice or potato part of the meal.

12 ounces rotelle

1 pound fresh spinach, thoroughly rinsed and tough stems removed

1/2 cup olive oil

4 anchovy filets, chopped into small, firm pieces

2 cloves garlic, minced

1/4 cup parsley, minced

1/4 cup pine nuts

Salt and pepper to taste

Cook pasta until al dente, drain well and mix with 1/4 cup olive oil. Do not refrigerate.

Slice spinach leaves crosswise into quarter-inch strips.

In a large frying pan, saute the anchovy filets, garlic and pine nuts in 1/4 cup olive oil until garlic and nuts are very lightly browned. Add spinach slices to the mixture and stir-fry until spinach is just wilted. Add contents of pan and the parsley to the rotelle, toss well, and add salt and pepper to taste. Serve at room temperature or slightly warm.

Serves 6.

Cold Vegetable and Rotini Salad

*A*rrange *the ingredients in layers in a large glass salad bowl and bring to the table so everyone can admire your salad before you toss it.*

8 ounces rotini

1/2 bunch broccoli, stems peeled

1 teaspoon dried tarragon leaves

1 package frozen snow peas, thawed only (or 8 ounces fresh snow peas, quickly blanched and drained)

8 ounces fresh green beans, sliced on the diagonal and quickly cooked until crisp-tender

4 carrots, cut in julienne strips

1 tablespoon fresh chives, snipped, or 1 teaspoon dried

4 scallions, cut into thin rounds, including green part

1/2 box cherry tomatoes, cut in half if large

1/2 cup chopped walnuts

Dressing

2/3 cup salad and olive oil mixture

1/2 cup fresh lemon juice

1/4 teaspoon dry mustard, or 1 teaspoon prepared Dijon mustard

Salt to taste (start with 1/2 teaspoon)

*C*ook rotini until al dente, drain well and toss with one tablespoon salad oil.

*C*ook broccoli in boiling salted water until crisp-tender. Drain and cool. Cut off florets; thinly slice stems.

*I*n large glass serving bowl, layer the broccoli sprinkled with the tarragon, the julienned carrots sprinkled with the chives, half the pasta, the green beans sprinkled with the scallions, the rest of the pasta, the cherry tomatoes, the snow peas, and the walnuts. Cover and chill.

*C*ombine the dressing ingredients and blend well. Pour over salad. Bring salad to table and toss.

*S*erves 6.

15

Caesar's Pasta

Recognize this old favorite? We hope you will enjoy the updated approach.

12 ounces vermicelli

1 garlic clove, lightly crushed

1 raw egg yolk

1 small bunch romaine lettuce, sliced narrowly crosswise

1 cup herb-flavored croutons

1/2 cup grated Parmesan cheese

Dressing

1/2 cup oil, half olive and half salad

1/4 cup lemon juice

1/2 tin anchovy fillets, lightly mashed (reserve other half)

1 teaspoon salt

1/2 teaspoon freshly ground pepper

1/4 teaspoon sugar

*R*ub a deep serving bowl with the crushed garlic clove.

*A*dd the egg yolk and mix lightly with a fork.

*C*ook the vermicelli until al dente, drain, rinse with cold water and drain thoroughly. Add to the bowl and toss with the egg.

*B*lend dressing ingredients in a small bowl.

*A*dd dressing, lettuce and 1/4 cup cheese and toss.

*T*op with croutons, reserved anchovies and remaining cheese and toss lightly.

*S*erves 6.

Twists and Eggplant

A favorite of an eggplant "freak" we know. Hearty enough to use as a main course but equally suitable for a first course. Makes a great leftover so don't worry about cutting back on amounts.

8 ounces small twist pasta or shells

1 large eggplant, peeled and diced

2 cups Italian plum tomatoes, chopped (save juice)

1 medium onion, chopped

1 cup celery, finely chopped

2 tablespoons minced parsley

2 cloves garlic, minced

1/2 cup olive oil, divided

1 teaspoon oregano

1/2 teaspoon thyme

Salt and freshly ground pepper to taste

Freshly grated Parmesan cheese to pass with pasta

Place the peeled and diced eggplant in a colander, sprinkle with salt and let sit for about 30 minutes.

Cook pasta until al dente, drain well and toss with 1 tablespoon olive oil. Transfer to a large serving bowl and set aside until sauce is ready.

Saute celery in 3 tablespoons heated olive oil for about 5 minutes. Add onion, parsley, garlic, oregano and thyme. Cook 5 minutes more.

Pat eggplant dry with a paper towel and saute in a large skillet in remaining olive oil until soft. Combine all the cooked vegetables and add the tomatoes with their juice. Bring to a boil, reduce heat, and cook at a low simmer for about ½ hour. Taste for seasonings. Cool slightly, then add to pasta; toss thoroughly. Serve at room temperature with Parmesan cheese.

Serves 6.

Eggplant and Linguine Salad

Here's a little different treatment for eggplant. If you want to be fancy about it, add about 1/4 cup of pine nuts to the eggplant during the last minute or two of cooking and brown lightly.

12 ounces linguine
1 eggplant, about 1 pound
2 tablespoons capers, rinsed and drained
3 cloves garlic, lightly crushed
1/2 cup olive oil, to start
Salt and pepper to taste

Cook pasta until al dente, drain well and toss with 1/4 cup olive oil. Set aside to cool.

Cut eggplant in half lengthwise and sprinkle heavily with salt; let stand 1/2 hour. (If eggplant is very young and fresh, this step can be omitted.) Rinse and dry eggplant, and cut into half-inch cubes.

In a large frying pan, saute the garlic in about 1/4 cup olive oil until lightly browned; discard garlic. Saute the cubed eggplant in the flavored oil over moderately high heat until browned; add more olive oil as necessary.

Toss the eggplant, capers and salt and pepper with the pasta. Let sit at least 1/2 hour so flavors can blend. Adjust seasonings before serving.

Serves 6.

Vegetables Vinaigrette with Rotelle

A *"good anytime" salad since the vegetables are available year round.*

8 ounces rotelle or any twist-type pasta
1/2 cauliflower
2 stalks broccoli
1 large carrot
1/2 pound green beans

Vinaigrette Dressing
1/4 cup olive oil, 2 tablespoons salad oil
3 teaspoons red wine vinegar
1 teaspoon Dijon mustard
1/2 cup chopped red onion
2 tablespoons chopped parsley
1/2 teaspoon dried basil, crushed

*B*reak cauliflower into florets and cook in boiling salted water barely 5 minutes. Drain, run under cold water and drain well.

*S*lice carrot into 1/2 inch rounds and cook 5 minutes in boiling salted water. Drain, run under cold water, and drain again.

*B*reak broccoli into florets (save stems for another use) and cook in boiling salted water barely 3 minutes. Drain, rinse with cold water and drain again.

*C*ombine vegetables and toss gently with prepared vinaigrette dressing. Refrigerate until 1/2 hour before serving.

*C*ook pasta until al dente, drain, rinse with cold water and drain again. Transfer to a large serving bowl and toss with additional 1/4 cup olive oil, 1 teaspoon red wine vinegar and 1/2 teaspoon salt. Cool to room temperature.

*T*oss pasta with marinated vegetables 1/2 hour before serving; do not refrigerate again.

*S*erves 6.

Winter Pasta Salad

We call this a winter salad because the vegetables it uses are sure to be available then. But because broccoli is available year round, you can make it at any season you choose.

8 ounces pasta twists

1 pound broccoli florets, lightly cooked until crisp-tender (about 3 minutes)

Approximately 9 ounces pickled Italian vegetables (giardinera), drained

1 small jar sliced pimiento, drained

Dressing

3/4 cup olive and salad oils mixed

3 tablespoons wine vinegar

1 clove garlic, minced

1 teaspoon egg yolk (optional—makes a creamier dressing)

1 teaspoon Dijon-style mustard

Salt and pepper to taste

Cook twists to al dente stage, drain well and toss with 1 tablespoon oil.

Mix twists with broccoli, pickled vegetables and pimiento.

To make sauce, mix together vinegar, garlic, optional egg yolk, and mustard. In blender or by hand using a whisk, slowly blend in oil, mixing well after each addition. Add salt and pepper to taste. Sauce should be fairly tart.

Add sauce to pasta and vegetable mixture, toss well, let stand at room temperature several hours so flavors can blend.

Serves 6.

A Pasta Salad with Character

This salad calls for a crunchy loaf of bread, a hearty jug of wine and at least six "thous" to share it.

12 ounces penne or elbow macaroni

1/2 box cherry tomatoes, halved

1/2 cup chopped parsley

1/2 cup cured black olives, Italian or Greek type

1 small red onion, thinly sliced

Dressing

3/4 cup olive oil

1/4 cup tarragon or basil vinegar

1 teaspoon crushed dried oregano

1/2 teaspoon dried basil or eight fresh basil leaves, chopped

1/4 teaspoon dried pepper flakes

4 cloves garlic, minced

1/4 cup capers, rinsed and drained

1 tin anchovy filets, drained and chopped

Cook pasta until al dente and drain well. Cool slightly in colander.

While pasta is cooking mix dressing ingredients in a small bowl.

Transfer pasta to a serving bowl and toss with about 1/2 cup dressing. Refrigerate if making early in the day but bring to room temperature before serving time. Add tomatoes, parsley, black olives, onions and remaining dressing to pasta. Toss gently before serving and taste for seasoning.

Serves 6.

Pickled Shells

_____

_____

_____

*F*or the pickle lovers in your family, this nicely old-fashioned salad is sure to please.

8 ounces pasta shells

1/2 cup sour cream

1/2 cup mayonnaise

2 tablespoons chopped onion

2 tablespoons chopped pimiento

2 tablespoons chopped parsley

1/4 teaspoon minced garlic

1/2 cup dill pickles, diced

2 tablespoons dill pickle juice, or as needed

Cook pasta shells to al dente stage, drain well. Toss with remaining ingredients, using the pickle juice as necessary to get the right consistency. Chill at least two hours.

Serves 6.

Low Salt, Low Fat Cold Pasta Salad (with Variations)

You don't have to be on a special diet to enjoy this salad. With the addition of the chicken or fish, it makes a satisfying and delicious main course. And you can vary the vegetables to suit what you have on hand.

8 ounces rotini or medium pasta shells

2 tomatoes, diced

4 scallions, diced

1 cucumber, peeled, seeded, and diced

1 red onion, diced

1 Spanish onion, diced

2 green and/or red peppers, seeded and diced

4 red potatoes, cooked and diced (do not peel)

1 bunch broccoli, briefly cooked and diced

1/2 pound green beans, briefly cooked and diced

1/4 cup parsley, minced

Fresh basil to taste, if available

Dressing

1/4 cup vinegar (balsamic or similar)

1/8 teaspoon Dijon mustard

Pinch oregano

1/2 teaspoon pepper

1 tablespoon frozen apple juice concentrate

Variations

1 pound boned and skinned chicken breasts, poached (covered) with 2 tablespoons dried basil leaves, then cooled and diced.

OR

1 pound salmon, sole or halibut filet, poached, cooled and flaked.

Cook pasta until al dente, drain well. Toss pasta with the vegetables (and chicken or fish, if desired). Vegetables can be prepared early in the day.

Shake dressing ingredients in covered jar until well blended, pour over other ingredients, and toss again. Serve at room temperature or lightly chilled.

Serves 6.

White Kidney Bean and Macaroni Salad Bibb

T his hearty salad could be a meal by itself. Or serve it with cold cuts and good rye bread for an easy meal after the big game.

8 ounces small, short macaroni

1 20-ounce can white kidney beans, rinsed and drained

1 cup mixed green and red sweet pepper (or all green), diced

1/4 cup fresh parsley, minced

2 cloves of garlic, minced

1 box small cherry tomatoes

1/2 cup of olive oil

4 tablespoons white wine vinegar

Salt and pepper to taste

_C_ook macaroni to al dente stage, drain well, and mix with 1 tablespoon olive oil to prevent sticking. Add vegetables and toss.

_I_n small jar shake oil, vinegar and salt and pepper together, pour over macaroni and vegetable mixture and toss thoroughly. Let stand so flavors can blend. Serve at room temperature or slightly chilled.

_S_erves 6.

Pasta Salad Nicoise

_____

_____

_____

All the wonderful flavor of the classic Nicoise salad but simpler to construct. Make early in the day or the day before to let the flavors "marry."

8 ounces rotelle, wheels or shell pasta

4 eggs, hard-cooked and sliced

2 tomatoes, diced

1 can anchovies

1/2 cup capers

1/2 cup black olives, sliced

2 red onions, coarsely chopped

2 pimientos, sliced

1/2 cup chopped parsley

Dressing

1/4 cup basil vinegar or white wine vinegar

1/2 cup olive oil

2 cloves garlic, minced

1 teaspoon salt or to taste

1/2 teaspoon freshly ground pepper

Cook pasta until al dente, drain, rinse under cold water and drain again. Toss with 1 tablespoon salad oil and set aside.

In a small bowl whisk together all dressing ingredients.

In a deep serving bowl put a layer of half the pasta, then a layer of eggs, tomatoes, anchovies, capers, olives, onions, pimientos and 1/4 cup parsley.

Sprinkle with half of the dressing.

Make a second layer of pasta, remaining half of the ingredients and sprinkle with the remaining dressing. Refrigerate until 1/2 hour before serving time. Toss very slightly before serving.

Serves 6.

Tomatoes Nicoise and Linguine

A *simple and simply delicious side dish. The perky dressing will even pep up winter tomatoes, but summer ones are best.*

12 ounces linguine	*Dressing*
3 tomatoes, peeled and thinly sliced	1/2 cup olive oil
12 Italian black olives	3 tablespoons red wine vinegar
1/4 cup freshly grated Parmesan cheese	4 anchovy fillets
1/4 cup chopped parsley	2 cloves garlic, minced
	1/4 teaspoon freshly ground pepper
	Salt to taste

*C*ook pasta until al dente, drain, rinse with cold water and drain again. Transfer to a serving bowl and toss with 1 tablespoon olive oil. Chill.

*M*ix all dressing ingredients in a medium bowl. Add the thinly sliced tomatoes and black olives. Marinate at room temperature at least 1 hour.

*M*ix the Parmesan cheese and chopped parsley and set aside. At serving time add the tomato mixture to the pasta and toss. Sprinkle with the cheese and parsley mixture and divide among 6 salad plates or bowls.

*S*erves 6.

Fettuccine and Tomatoes in Lemon Sauce

This fresh-tasting salad will sharpen jaded summer appetites. To keep the lemon theme going, serve the salad with chicken pieces marinated in lemon and oil and grilled on the barbecue.

1 pound fettuccine, fresh if desired

4-6 ripe tomatoes, diced

6-8 fresh basil leaves

Juice of 1 lemon

6 tablespoons olive oil

Salt and pepper to taste

Cook fettuccine to the al dente stage, drain well. Toss with the oil, lemon juice, and salt and pepper to taste. Toss again with the tomatoes and basil. Adjust seasonings and serve warm or at room temperature.

Serves 6.

Garden Fresh Pasta Salad

A melange of the freshest summer vegetables and a simple-to-make pesto sauce result in an easy and vitamin-packed main dish.

8 ounces rigatoni or other large tube pasta

Sliced and cubed fresh vegetables to equal 4 cups: green beans, zucchini, yellow squash, eggplant, red or green peppers

2 cups packed fresh basil leaves

1/4 cup good olive oil

1/4 cup salad oil

1/4 cup pine nuts or coarsely chopped walnuts

3 cloves garlic, minced

1 teaspoon salt

1/2 teaspoon freshly ground pepper

1/2 cup freshly grated Parmesan cheese

1/4 cup freshly grated Romano or pecorino cheese

Cherry tomatoes

*P*ut the basil leaves, olive oil and salt into a blender or food processor and blend just until combined but not pureed.

*I*n a small skillet heat the 1/4 cup salad oil and lightly brown the pine nuts. Add the garlic and let it barely color.

*C*ook the pasta until al dente and drain. Transfer to a serving bowl and toss with the oil and pine nuts and freshly ground pepper.

*I*n a large pot of boiling salted water cook the beans about 3 minutes, add the squash and eggplant and cook an additional 3 minutes. Drain and plunge into cold water to stop the cooking and retain the color. Drain thoroughly.

*A*dd cooked vegetables to the pasta along with the pesto sauce and toss gently. Add the cheeses and cherry tomatoes and toss again. Serve at room temperature.

*S*erves 6.

Vegetable and Pasta Salad with Pizazz

_____

_____

_____

*S*_pice up an otherwise ordinary meal with a side dish of snappy salad served at room temperature. It's equally good summer or winter._

12 ounces fettuccine

3 cups chopped broccoli, cooked 2 minutes until crisp

1 pint cherry tomatoes, halved

1/3 cup olive oil

3 garlic cloves, minced

1/2 cup chopped onions

2 tablespoons fresh basil, chopped, or 2 teaspoons dried basil, crushed

1/2 teaspoon red pepper flakes, or more to taste

1 teaspoon salt

1/2 teaspoon freshly ground pepper

1/2 cup freshly grated Parmesan cheese

*C*ook fettuccine until al dente and drain. In a serving bowl, toss pasta with 1 tablespoon olive oil and 1/2 teaspoon salt.

*H*eat 1/3 cup oil in a large skillet and saute onions until tender. Add garlic and basil and cook briefly. Add tomatoes, cook about 2 minutes, then sprinkle with the salt and pepper.

*R*emove pan from the heat and cool mixture a bit. Very gently stir in the cooked broccoli and red pepper flakes. Add to the pasta and toss at the table. Pass the Parmesan cheese separately.

*S*erves 6.

Roasted Pepper, Zucchini and Pasta Salad

A year-round salad. The jarred roast peppers are a tasty substitute for the fresh variety. The bright green and red colors would be an appealing addition to a Christmas buffet table.

8 ounces rotelle or penne

3 medium zucchini

3 red peppers roasted, or a 7-ounce jar roasted peppers, drained

5 cloves garlic, minced

1/2 cup oil, half olive and half salad

1-1/2 teaspoons oregano, crushed

3 tablespoons chopped parsley

2 teaspoons salt

3/4 teaspoon freshly ground pepper

3 tablespoons white wine vinegar

Cook the pasta until al dente and drain. Transfer to a large bowl and toss with 1 tablespoon oil.

Halve the zucchini lengthwise and slice into 1/4 inch pieces. Salt lightly and let drain for 30 minutes. Pat dry.

Meanwhile, if using fresh red peppers, roast them under a preheated broiler until all sides are charred. Wrap in tinfoil or close up in a brown paper bag. When cool, slip off charred skins, remove seeds and cut in narrow strips. Cut drained, jarred peppers into narrow strips.

Heat 1/4 cup oil in a large skillet and saute the zucchini for no more than 2 minutes. Remove with a slotted spoon to a bowl.

Add the remaining oil and garlic to the skillet and cook over low heat about 1 minute or until the garlic lightly browns. Add the oregano and pour oil mixture over the roasted peppers. Add the parsley, salt, pepper, and vinegar. Stir and add to the cooled pasta. Toss lightly and add the zucchini but do not toss until ready to serve. This will prevent the zucchini from turning an off shade of green.

Refrigerate until 30 minutes before serving time.

Serves 6.

Artichoke and Pasta Salad with Tomato Sauce

An easy side dish to accompany grilled rosemary chicken, broiled fish or just a plain hamburger.

8 ounces ziti

1 6-ounce jar marinated artichoke hearts

1/2 cup chopped onions

2 cloves garlic, minced

2 cups peeled and diced tomatoes or
1 16-ounce can Italian plum tomatoes,
drained and chopped

1 bay leaf

1 teaspoon salt

Freshly ground pepper to taste

1/2 teaspoon oregano, crushed

1/4 teaspoon marjoram, crushed

1/2 teaspoon basil, crushed, or
1 tablespoon fresh, chopped

2 tablespoons chopped parsley

1/4 cup olive oil

1/2 cup grated Parmesan cheese

Cook pasta until al dente and drain. Transfer to a serving bowl and toss with 1/4 cup olive oil.

Drain marinade from the artichokes into a 10-inch skillet. Set the artichokes aside. Add the garlic and onions to the liquid and simmer until the onions become translucent. Add the tomatoes, bay leaf, herbs and salt. Cover and simmer 10 minutes. Uncover and cook another 10 minutes. Cut the artichokes in half and add to the tomato sauce. Heat for a few minutes. Remove the bay leaf and stir in the parsley. Cool to room temperature and pour over the pasta. Toss until well blended. Pass the Parmesan cheese separately.

Serves 6.

Fettuccine and Mushroom Salad

An almost traditional pasta first course, with a twist: this pasta in a creamy sauce is served cold.

12 ounces fettuccine
8 large mushrooms (about 1/4 pound)
4 green onions
1/3 cup grated Parmesan cheese
1/4 cup minced parsley
1/2 cup heavy cream
3 tablespoons olive oil
3 tablespoons tarragon or basil vinegar
Salt and freshly ground pepper to taste
1/2 teaspoon crushed tarragon

Cook pasta until al dente, drain well and toss with 1 tablespoon olive oil.

Thinly slice mushrooms and green onions and place in a large shallow serving bowl; add all remaining ingredients except the fettuccine. Mix thoroughly. Add the pasta but do not toss. Cover with plastic wrap and chill for several hours.

Bring to room temperature and toss before serving.

Taste for seasonings and divide among 6 salad plates.

Serves 6.

Broccoli, Walnut Primavera

*P*rimavera means "springtime" but this variation has year-round appeal. When fresh basil is not available for the dressing, substitute fresh spinach and dried basil.

12 ounces fettuccini

2 large ripe tomatoes, or 1 basket cherry tomatoes

1 bunch broccoli

1/2 can pitted black olives, sliced

1/2 cup coarsely chopped walnuts

Dressing

2 cups fresh basil leaves (or fresh spinach and 2 teaspoons dried basil)

2/3 cup olive oil

2 cloves garlic

1/4 cup grated Parmesan cheese

1/4 cup chopped walnuts

1/4 cup red wine vinegar

1 teaspoon salt

1/4 teaspoon freshly ground pepper

*C*ook pasta until al dente, drain, rinse with cold water and drain thoroughly. Place in a large shallow bowl. Mix with 1 tablespoon olive oil.

*S*eed tomatoes and chop coarsely, or halve cherry tomatoes. Slice peeled broccoli stems 1/4 inch thick and break florets into smaller pieces. Cook 3 minutes in boiling salted water. Drain, rinse with cold water and drain again.

*A*dd tomatoes, broccoli, olives and walnuts to the pasta and toss gently.

*I*n a blender or food processor chop the basil (spinach), garlic, walnuts, Parmesan cheese and vinegar. Add the olive oil in a slow stream until it is all absorbed. Stir in the salt and pepper.

*P*our 1/2 cup dressing over the salad and toss thoroughly but gently. Pass additional sauce and Parmesan cheese at the table. Serve slightly chilled or at room temperature.

*S*erves 6.

Pasta Primavera, Again

There are endless versions of pasta primavera and we love them all; here is still another. Enjoy.

12 ounces linguine or fettuccine

1 pound zucchini

1/2 bunch (about 1/2 pound) broccoli

1/2 pound green beans

1/4 cup salad oil

6 shallots or 4 scallions, white part only

2 cloves garlic, minced

1/4 cup chopped parsley

2 tablespoons fresh basil, chopped, or
2 teaspoons dried, crushed, or 1 teaspoon
pesto sauce

1 teaspoon salt and freshly ground pepper

2 tablespoons olive oil

1/4 cup light cream

1/2 cup freshly grated Parmesan cheese

Cook pasta until al dente and drain. Transfer to a shallow bowl and toss with 2 tablespoons olive oil and 1/4 cup light cream. Cool but do not refrigerate.

Wash and trim all vegetables and chop into rather small pieces.

Heat 1/4 cup oil in a large skillet that has a cover. Add the vegetables, and stir to coat with oil. Add the shallots and garlic. Cover and steam over high heat for 5 minutes. Uncover and add the basil and parsley and stir well. Cook slightly longer; the vegetables should be crunchy.

Season vegetables with the salt and pepper and add to the pasta. Toss well and let come to room temperature.

Sprinkle with the Parmesan cheese before serving.

Serves 6.

Crunchy and Creamy Curried Pasta Salad

*A*dd some zest to that simple sandwich meal you're planning after a hard day's work or a lazy day at the beach.

8 ounces shells, wheels or macaroni

1 green or red pepper, roughly chopped

1/2 cup sliced celery

6 green onions, cut into 1/2 inch slices

1 small jar pimiento, drained and chopped

1/4 cup chopped parsley

Dressing

1/2 cup mayonnaise

1/2 cup sour cream

2 tablespoons olive oil

2 tablespoons vinegar

2 teaspoons curry powder

1 teaspoon salt

1/4 teaspoon pepper

*C*ook pasta until al dente, drain, rinse under cold water and drain thoroughly.

*M*ix with 1 tablespoon oil and refrigerate while preparing vegetables and blending dressing ingredients.

*T*oss all vegetables and dressing with cold pasta and chill thoroughly. Prepare early in the day if possible.

*S*erves 6.

Ultra-Simple Green Pasta Salad

An almost instant side dish to serve with a wide variety of meat, poultry or seafood main dishes.

12 ounces green fettuccine

1 4-ounce jar whole pimientos, cut in strips

1/2 cup chopped green onions (including tops)

1/4 cup chopped parsley

1/3 cup toasted sunflower seeds, unsalted

2 tablespoons olive oil

1 tablespoon vinegar

1/4 teaspoon salt

1/4 teaspoon freshly ground pepper

1/2 teaspoon dried oregano, crushed

1/4 cup mayonnaise

1/4 cup sour cream or plain yogurt

1/2 teaspoon salt

1/4 teaspoon freshly ground pepper

Cook fettuccine until al dente and drain. Rinse under cold water and drain again. Transfer to a serving bowl and toss with the olive oil, vinegar, 1/4 teaspoon salt and 1/4 teaspoon freshly ground pepper, oregano, pimientos, green onions and parsley.

Mix the mayonnaise and sour cream and remaining salt and pepper together and add to the pasta with the sunflower seeds; toss again.

Serves 6.

Linguine Salad Foster

This simple-seeming salad is really quite sophisticated in flavor. It's a wonderful start to a meal that's based on the flavors of the Mediterranean.

12 ounces linguine
1/4 pound cured black olives, pitted
1 tin flat anchovy filets, drained
1/4 cup minced parsley
1/4 cup olive oil, or more as necessary
Freshly ground black pepper

Cook pasta until al dente, drain well, and toss with 1/4 cup olive oil. Set aside to cool completely.

Slice the pitted olives into thin strips. Chop the anchovies into small, firm pieces; do not mash.

Toss the pasta with the olives and anchovies. Let sit for at least 1/2 hour so flavors can blend. Just before serving, toss again with the parsley, freshly ground black pepper to taste, and a little additional olive oil.

Serves 6.

Sweet and Sour Orzo and Vegetable Salad

*T*his combination makes a refreshing first course or side dish with baked ham or deli sandwiches.

1-1/2 cups orzo

1 cup seeded, peeled cucumber, chopped

1 cup chopped carrots

1/2 cup chopped green onions

Lettuce leaves for garnish

Dressing

1/2 cup white wine vinegar

2 tablespoons oil

3 tablespoons sugar

1 tablespoon chopped fresh dill or
1 teaspoon dried dillweed

1 teaspoon salt

1/4 teaspoon ground red pepper

1/4 cup toasted sesame seeds for garnish

*C*ook pasta until al dente, drain, rinse with cold water and drain thoroughly. Refrigerate.

*P*repare vegetables and dressing. Add to cold pasta and gently stir to mix. Cover and refrigerate until serving time, at least 1 hour.

*L*ine a serving bowl with lettuce leaves and mound salad on top; sprinkle with sesame seeds. Or place lettuce and salad on individual salad plates and serve as a first course.

*S*erves 6.

Mystery Garden Pasta Salad

This is easy and quick and fun to serve. Your family or guests will be hard-pressed to identify the mystery ingredient.

12 ounces linguine
1/2 pound broccoli
5 medium carrots
4 quarts boiling water
1 teaspoon salt
12 cherry tomatoes, halved
1/2 cup chopped green onions
2 tablespoons sesame seeds

Dressing
1/2 cup wheat germ, whirled in a blender or processor until fine
3/4 cup salad oil
1 teaspoon sesame oil
1/2 cup lemon juice
4 tablespoons soy sauce
2 cloves garlic

*A*dd all the dressing ingredients to the wheat germ and process 30 seconds.

*P*eel broccoli stems and slice 1/4 inch thick. Break heads into small florets. Peel and thinly slice carrots. Break linguini into 3-inch pieces.

*A*dd the linguine to the boiling, salted water and cook 3 minutes. Add broccoli and carrots and cook 2 minutes longer. Drain, rinse with cold water and drain thoroughly again. Transfer to a large serving bowl and toss gently with about 1/2 cup dressing. Refrigerate.

*B*efore serving add tomatoes, green onions and sesame seeds and drizzle with more dressing to taste.

Serves 6.

Sesame Pasta Salad

This pasta salad, a variation of one served by Washington, D.C.'s American Cafe, can be addictive. And it's so simple to make, you'll be able to satisfy your craving often.

12 ounces linguine

1/4 cup Chinese sesame oil

4 tablespoons soy sauce

1/2 teaspoon minced garlic

1/2 cup minced watercress

1 teaspoon hot chili oil (or to taste)

Salt and freshly ground black pepper to taste

Cook linguine to al dente stage, drain well and toss with remaining ingredients. Chill salad for several hours and preferably overnight.

Serves 6.

Szechuan Dan Dan Noodles

*W*e are providing a number of sesame and noodle recipes to let you discover *your favorite—as well as the one that calls for ingredients available in your area.*

1 pound vermicelli or linguine

2 tablespoons salad oil

Dressing

1/2 cup sesame seeds, toasted and crushed

1/2 cup scallions, minced, green included

2 cloves garlic, minced

2 tablespoons grated fresh ginger

2 tablespoons Chinese sesame oil

1/2 cup red wine vinegar

2 teaspoons sugar

1 teaspoon hot chili oil

1 teaspoon Szechuan peppercorns, crushed in a mortar, if available

1/2 cup cilantro (Chinese parsley) coarsely chopped, if available

*C*ook the pasta until al dente, drain well, and toss with the salad oil.

*M*ix the dressing ingredients together. Adjust the seasonings. You may want to add the hot chili oil and the pepper a little at a time until it suits your taste.

*T*oss the pasta with the dressing; garnish with additional cilantro leaves and sliced scallion if desired. Serve at room temperature or chilled.

*S*erves 6.

Sutton Place Gourmet Oriental Pasta Salad

*T*he *Sutton Place Gourmet of Washington, D.C. feels that the complementary flavors of rich, nutty whole wheat pasta and crunchy oriental vegetables make this unique salad a vegetarian delight. The addition of protein-rich tofu makes it nutritious as well as delicious.*

12 ounces whole wheat fusilli, fresh if possible

4 green onions, green part only, sliced

1 small bottle baby corn, drained

1 8-ounce can bamboo shoots, drained, rinsed and sliced

1 8-ounce can water chestnuts, drained, rinsed and sliced

1 cup shredded carrots

1/2 pound tofu, cubed (optional)

1/4 cup sesame oil

1/4 cup soy sauce

*C*ook the pasta until al dente, drain, rinse with cold water and drain again. Transfer to a large bowl and toss with 1 tablespoon sesame oil.

*M*ix the remaining sesame oil and the soy sauce in a small bowl.

*A*dd the remaining ingredients to the pasta, pour the dressing over and toss to coat thoroughly.

*S*erve at room temperature.

*S*erves 6.

Ginger and Scallion Lo Mein Salad

A good accompaniment for chicken or duck roasted and basted with a soy sauce marinade.

1 pound thin egg noodles, fresh if possible

1-inch portion fresh ginger, peeled and minced

1 bunch scallions, coarsely chopped

1 tablespoon vegetable oil

1/2 cup chicken broth

1 teaspoon sugar

2 tablespoons soy sauce

2 tablespoons hoisin sauce

2 tablespoons sesame oil

Cook noodles until al dente, drain, rinse with cold water, drain well. Toss with the sesame oil.

Stir-fry ginger and scallions in the vegetable oil briefly. Add rest of ingredients, mix well.

Toss noodles with the sauce mixture. Add a little more sesame oil if necessary. Let come to room temperature and serve.

Serves 6.

Simple Oriental Noodle Salad

This salad is as uncluttered as a Japanese home and each flavor is distinct on the palate.

12 ounces rice sticks or capellini

4 tablespoons olive oil

2 tablespoons sesame oil

2 tablespoons sesame-chili oil

4 tablespoons rice vinegar

1/2 teaspoon salt or more to taste

1 tablespoon toasted sesame seeds

2/3 cup finely snipped chives or finely chopped green onion tops

1/3 cup finely chopped parsley

Cook pasta until al dente, drain thoroughly. Toss with the olive, sesame and sesame-chili oils and the rice vinegar. Cover with plastic wrap and chill for several hours or overnight.

Just before serving, add sesame seeds, chives and parsley and toss lightly. Adjust seasoning if necessary.

Serves 6.

Fettuccine in Walnut Sauce

A *good first course. It looks especially nice served on a large platter surrounded by a vegetable salad of cherry tomatoes, sliced Jerusalem artichokes, and green pepper squares dressed in a basic vinaigrette.*

12 ounces fettuccine

1 small bunch parsley, washed and stems removed

8 ounces shelled walnuts

3 garlic cloves, minced

1 cup olive oil

1 teaspoon salt

1/2 teaspoon freshly ground pepper

*C*ook fettuccine until al dente, drain well and toss with 2 tablespoons olive oil.

*I*n blender or food processor, whirl parsley, walnuts, garlic with the olive oil added in a slow stream. Add salt and pepper and blend again.

*T*oss fettuccine and 1/2 cup walnut sauce. Chill to allow flavors to blend. Add more sauce if the pasta has absorbed too much of the sauce and is dry. May be served chilled or at room temperature.

*S*erves 6.

San Remo Pasta Salad, Fete Accomplie

Quite elegant in its simplicity, this salad from Fete Accomplie Catering of Washington, D.C. will be a perfect side-dish for many of your grilled meat, fish and poultry entrees.

12 ounces fusilli
1/2 cup chopped sun-dried tomatoes
1/2 cup chopped fresh basil
1/2 cup freshly grated Parmesan cheese
1/2 cup black Italian or Greek olives
1/3 cup oil from dried tomatoes
1/3 cup salad oil
2 tablespoons basil vinegar
1/2 teaspoon salt or more to taste
1/2 teaspoon freshly ground black pepper

Cook pasta until al dente, drain, rinse with cold water and drain again.

Add all remaining ingredients and toss lightly. Taste for seasoning and adjust to taste.

Serve at room temperature or lightly chilled.

Serves 6.

Tortellini Salad

*E*asy to do because the tortellini can be purchased from an Italian grocery store or in the frozen-food section of most supermarkets. Check the Italian market for some fresh, crisp arugola for the salad and a crunchy bread to round out the meal.

1 pound meat- or cheese-filled tortellini or agnolotti

2 red peppers or 1 small jar whole pimientos

1/2 cup chopped green onions

1/2 cup cured Italian black olives

1/2 cup toasted chopped walnuts

Dressing

1 cup olive oil or half olive and half salad

1/3 cup wine vinegar

2 teaspoons Dijon mustard

2 tablespoons chopped parsley

2 tablespoons chopped fresh dill or 1 teaspoon dried dillweed

1 tablespoon fresh oregano or 1 teaspoon dried oregano, crushed

1 teaspoon salt

1/2 teaspoon freshly ground black pepper

*C*ook the pasta in boiling salted water, 5 to 10 minutes for fresh, 10 to 15 minutes for frozen. Test before draining. Drain and rinse with cold water and drain thoroughly. Toss gently with 2 tablespoons oil and cool.

*S*lice the peppers or pimientos into thin strips.

*R*inse the cured olives and drain.

*M*ix all the dressing ingredients thoroughly. (This is more dressing than you will use but it's delicious on any salad.)

*I*n a large bowl carefully mix the pasta, peppers, onions, olives, walnuts and 1/2 cup of the dressing. Cover and chill a few hours. Before serving taste for salt and pepper and add more dressing if salad is a bit dry.

*S*erves 6.

Agnolotti and Tomato Salad

Unfortunately, summer is really the only time to savor this salad. Fresh tomatoes and basil are absolutely essential to the finished product. Worth waiting for.

1 pound agnolotti or tortellini, meat or cheese filled

2 pounds small tomatoes, cut into thin wedges

1/2 pound whole-milk mozzarella, cut into 1/4 inch slices and quartered

1 cup Italian cured black olives (or Nicoise if available)

1/4 cup finely chopped parsley, for garnish

Dressing

3/4 cup good olive oil

1/4 cup white wine or basil vinegar

2 tablespoons minced fresh basil

1 teaspoon salt

Freshly ground pepper to taste (use a lot)

Cook the pasta in boiling salted water 5 to 10 minutes if fresh and 10 to 15 minutes if frozen; test before draining. Drain, rinse under cold water and drain again. Transfer to a large bowl and toss with 1 tablespoon oil.

Add the tomato wedges, mozzarella slices and olives to the pasta.

Beat the dressing ingredients together in a small bowl until well combined.

Drizzle dressing over the salad and toss gently. Serve at room temperature for maximum flavor but chilled is almost as good.

Serves 6.

Rotelle, Mushrooms and Broccoli with a Creamy Tomato Sauce

_____

_____

_____

*H*ere *is a satisfying side dish to accompany any grilled or broiled meat: lamb chops, rosemary chicken or assorted sauteed sausages, for example.*

8 ounces rotelle

1 pound mushrooms, quartered

1-1/2 cups broccoli, coarsely chopped and blanched

3 tablespoons olive oil

1 cup light cream

1 cup canned plum tomatoes, drained and coarsely chopped

1 teaspoon crushed dried oregano

1 teaspoon crushed dried basil

1/2 teaspoon salt or more to taste

1/2 teaspoon freshly ground pepper

Freshly grated Parmesan cheese to pass separately

*C*ook pasta until al dente, drain and toss with 1 tablespoon olive oil.

*H*eat 3 tablespoons olive oil in a large skillet, add the mushrooms and saute quickly over high heat until golden.

*R*emove from heat and add cream, tomatoes and seasonings. Mix well and cool to room temperature.

*T*oss the mushroom, tomato and cream mixture with the pasta.

*A*dd the broccoli just before serving and toss gently again. Taste for seasonings.

*S*erve at room temperature and pass the grated Parmesan separately.

*S*erves 6.

Shells, Peas and Banana Peppers

The yellow pepper rings and the fresh green peas add colorful—and tasty— accents to this simple salad.

8 ounces shell pasta	*Dressing*
1 pound fresh peas, shelled and blanched	1/2 cup olive oil
3 long yellow peppers, sliced in thin rings	1/3 cup basil vinegar
1/4 pound fontina cheese, cut into thin slivers	1 teaspoon crushed dried basil or 1 tablespoon minced fresh basil
2 cloves garlic, minced	1 teaspoon salt
1/4 cup chopped parsley	1/2 teaspoon freshly ground black pepper

*C*ook pasta until al dente, drain, rinse with cold water and drain again. Mix with 1 tablespoon olive oil.

*P*lunge shelled peas for about 1 minute into 1 quart boiling water. Drain and dry with paper toweling.

*A*dd peas, sliced peppers, cheese and garlic to pasta in serving bowl. Add 1/2 cup dressing and toss, taste for seasoning. Add remaining dressing just before serving. Serve at room temperature or lightly chilled.

*S*erves 6.

Linguine with Artichoke, Basil and Walnut Sauce

*F*resh basil is a must for this salad but frozen artichoke hearts simplify the preparations.

12 ounces spinach linguine

1/2 cup olive oil, divided

1 9-ounce package frozen artichoke hearts, thawed and quartered

4 garlic cloves, minced

1/2 cup coarsely chopped walnuts

1/2 cup fresh basil leaves, minced

1/2 cup chopped parsley

1 teaspoon oregano

1 teaspoon salt

1/2 teaspoon freshly ground black pepper

*C*ook pasta until al dente, drain and toss with 2 tablespoons olive oil.

*H*eat remaining oil and add artichoke hearts and saute until golden; add garlic and walnuts and saute until walnuts color slightly. Remove from heat.

*A*dd the basil, parsley, oregano, salt and pepper; mix well and let cool without refrigerating.

*T*oss with the pasta and serve at room temperature.

*S*erves 6.

Not Low-Cal Pasta, Mushroom and Pepper Salad

We can't be good all the time. Just enjoy and diet tomorrow.

12 ounces spinach tagliatelle

1/2 pound mushrooms, thinly sliced

2 green peppers, cored, seeded and thinly sliced

2 red peppers, cored, seeded and thinly sliced

1/4 cup chopped parsley

Dressing

1/2 cup lemon juice, divided

1 cup mayonnaise

1 cup creme fraiche

1/4 cup tarragon vinegar

2 tablespoons crushed dried basil

2 teaspoons crushed dried tarragon

1 teaspoon salt or more to taste

1/2 teaspoon freshly ground black pepper or more to taste

Marinate the mushrooms in 1/4 cup lemon juice overnight.

Early in the day, cook the pasta until al dente, drain, rinse under cold water and drain again.

Drain mushrooms and discard juice.

Combine mayonnaise, creme fraiche, mushrooms, vinegar, herbs, salt and pepper.

Add green and red pepper slices and parsley to pasta. Add dressing and mix gently but thoroughly. (You may not need to use all the dressing.) Cover with plastic wrap and chill at least 4 hours before serving.

Serves 6.

Capellini with Broccoli and Goat Cheese

*H*ere *is a first course that might be followed by quickly grilled fish fillets flavored with lemon and rosemary, small new potatoes rolled in crumbs and sauteed in garlic butter and a crisp salad of arugola with a mild vinaigrette dressing.*

12 ounces capellini or vermicelli
1-1/2 cups small broccoli florets
1/2 cup olive oil, divided
1/2 teaspoon thyme, crushed
1 clove garlic, minced
1/2 teaspoon salt
1/4 pound goat cheese, cut into slivers
Freshly ground black pepper

*C*ook the pasta until al dente, drain and toss with 1 tablespoon olive oil.

*H*eat the remaining oil in a small skillet and add the broccoli florets, thyme, garlic and salt. Toss broccoli to coat in oil and heat briefly; it should remain crisp.

*R*emove from heat and toss with the pasta. Cool to room temperature.

*J*ust before serving add goat cheese and freshly ground black pepper to taste. Divide among six salad plates.

*S*erves 6.

Vegetarian Pasta Salad La Prima

L a Prima gourmet shops in Houston, Dallas and Washington, D.C. feature this snappy salad.

8 ounces rotelle or rotini

1/2 cup green beans, julienned in 1-1/2 inch lengths

1/2 cup zucchini, halved lengthwise and sliced across

1/2 cup chopped sweet pickles

1/4 cup chopped Bermuda onion

2 tablespoons capers, rinsed and drained

1/4 cup small pitted black olives

Dressing

3/4 cup mayonnaise

2 tablespoons lemon juice

1 tablespoon olive oil

1/2 teaspoon salt

1/2 teaspoon freshly ground black pepper

*C*ook pasta until al dente, drain, rinse with cold water and drain again. Toss with 1 tablespoon oil.

*B*lanch green beans for 2 minutes in boiling water, drain, rinse with cold water and drain again.

*M*ix dressing ingredients in a small bowl.

*A*dd beans, zucchini, chopped pickles, onion, capers and black olives to pasta in a large serving bowl.

*A*dd the dressing and mix gently but thoroughly. Taste for seasoning. Chill at least 2 hours before serving.

Serves 6.

Mostaciolli and Broccoli with Creamy Garlic Sauce

What could be simpler? Cook the pasta, blanch the broccoli and whirl the dressing ingredients in a blender. Then serve and enjoy.

8 ounces mostaciolli
1 pound broccoli
1 recipe Creamy Garlic Sauce, page 168

Cook pasta until al dente, drain, rinse with cold water and drain again. Mix with 1/4 cup of the Creamy Garlic Sauce.

Discard heavy bottom stems of broccoli. Peel remaining stems and slice 1/4 inch thick. Break florets of broccoli into smaller pieces. Blanch stems and florets about 2 minutes in boiling water. Drain, rinse with cold water and drain again. Pat dry with paper towels. Add to pasta in serving bowl and toss with 1/2 cup (or more) of the dressing.

Serve at room temperature or lightly chilled.

Serves 6.

Marinated Vegetables with Unadorned Pasta

The ultimate dieter's treat that is very low in calories, filling and nutritious.

8 ounces rotelle

3 carrots, diced

1 large zucchini, diced

1 cup coarsely chopped cauliflower

1/4 cup diced green pepper

1/4 cup chopped green onions

4 radishes, sliced

12 to 15 cherry tomatoes, halved

Dressing

1 cup low fat yogurt

1/4 cup dry white wine

2 cloves garlic, minced

1 teaspoon dry mustard

1 teaspoon dried oregano, crushed

1/2 teaspoon dried basil, crushed

Cook the rotelle until al dente, drain and rinse with cold water and drain again. Cover and refrigerate.

Mix dressing ingredients in a small bowl.

Prepare vegetables and mix with the dressing. Refrigerate several hours or overnight.

To serve, arrange the pasta in a shallow bowl and top with the vegetables; do not toss.

Serves 6.

Healthful Vegetable and Orzo Salad

Another dieter's delight—lots of color, texture and flavor but few calories.

1 cup orzo, ave maria or other tiny pasta

1/2 cup coarsely chopped green or red pepper

1/4 cup chopped radishes

1/2 cup peeled, seeded and chopped cucumber

2 tablespoons chopped parsley

Dressing

1/2 cup plain low fat yogurt

3 tablespoons cider vinegar

1 tablespoon lemon juice

1/2 package or 1/8 teaspoon powdered artificial sweetener

2 teaspoons curry powder

Cook pasta until al dente, drain, rinse and drain well again. Add vegetables and mix well.

Mix dressing ingredients in a small bowl and add to the pasta and vegetables. Mix lightly.

Cover and refrigerate for at least 6 hours or overnight.

Serves 6.

Almost Classic Pasta Salad

We think you will enjoy this variation of the dependable macaroni salad recipe that we all seem to have in our files.

8 ounces shell or wheel pasta

2 tablespoons lemon juice

1 tablespoon olive oil

1/4 cup chopped green onions

1 cup chopped celery with leaves

1/2 cup chopped parsley

1/2 cup sliced pimiento stuffed olives

1/4 cup chopped green pepper

2 hard-cooked eggs, coarsely chopped (optional)

2 tablespoons sunflower seeds (optional)

1/4 cup mayonnaise

1/4 cup sour cream

1 teaspoon salt

1/2 teaspoon freshly ground black pepper

1 tablespoon white vinegar

Cook pasta until al dente and drain well. In a large serving bowl mix the lemon juice and olive oil. Add the pasta, toss and refrigerate, covered, at least 1 hour.

Mix the mayonnaise, sour cream, vinegar and seasonings in a small bowl.

At serving time add the vegetables and optional eggs and sunflower seeds to the pasta. Add the dressing and mix thoroughly. Taste for seasoning.

Serves 6.

Pasta Salad Bar

A *wonderful idea for a buffet: Let your guests create their own pasta salads using their favorite ingredients. Provide plates or shallow bowls large enough to allow mixing. Set up the buffet table with a large bowl of pasta tossed with olive oil and smaller bowls containing other ingredients and pitchers of sauces and dressings. Below are some suggestions; amounts aren't given—that will depend on the number of guests and their appetites. Interesting breads, a choice of either red or white wine and a fabulous dessert complete the meal. It's fun.*

Pasta

Twists, shells or ribbon-type pasta broken into shorter lengths for easier handling, cooked al dente, drained well and tossed with 2 tablespoons olive oil for each pound of pasta

Toppings

Scallions, chopped

Garlic, minced

Parsley, minced

Capers, rinsed and drained

Green olives

Black olives

Walnuts

Pine nuts

Mozzarella or other mild cheese, julienned

Parmesan cheese, grated

Feta cheese, crumbled

Green or red sweet peppers, julienned

Broccoli florets

Green beans, halved and blanched

Cucumbers, peeled, seeded and diced

Cherry tomatoes, halved

Chick peas, rinsed and drained

Pepperoni or salami, julienned

Roast beef, julienned

Chicken breast, poached and shredded

Tuna fish, drained and chunked

Shellfish, such as shrimp, lobster, scallops, cooked and cut into small pieces

Flat anchovies, cut into tiny pieces

Dressings

Creamy Garlic Sauce (page 168)

Parsley Pesto (page 169)

Sesame Seed Vinaigrette (page 163)

Basic Vinaigrette (page 160)

Pasta Salads with Poultry

Pasta Salads with Poultry

Chicken and pasta seem to have a special affinity for each other in salads—maybe because each takes so well to having its own special flavor enhanced by seasonings and sauces.

Use either boned and skinned chicken breasts—sometimes called chicken cutlets—or bone-in chicken breast halves; the boned weight should equal about a pound. For perfectly poached chicken breasts, keep the water below the simmer (a slight surface shimmering is ideal); that way, the meat turns out juicy and succulent; high heat tends to produce stringy and dry chicken.

Indonesian Spaghetti and Chicken Salad

An exotic-sounding recipe that's both simple to make and delicious. The dressing ingredients can be found at oriental food stores and in the gourmet section of most supermarkets.

8 ounces dried oriental whole wheat noodles or the same amount of thin spaghetti

1 whole chicken breast, boned and skinned

1 pound fresh peas, shelled or 1 10-oz package frozen peas, thawed

1/4 pound radishes, sliced

2 cucumbers, peeled

Dressing

1/3 cup peanut butter

6 tablespoons soy sauce

3 tablespoons vinegar

10 drops hot chili oil

12 drops sesame oil

1/8 cup water

Cook oriental noodles for 4 minutes in boiling water or if using spaghetti, until al dente, drain, rinse with cold water and drain again; do not refrigerate.

Poach the chicken breast in a small amount of water for about 20 minutes. Cool and cut into strips, 1-1/2 x 1/2 inches. Cut cucumbers in half lengthwise and remove seeds. Slice into 1/8-inch half-rounds.

Parboil fresh peas or pour boiling water over thawed frozen peas; drain thoroughly.

In a large bowl combine noodles, chicken, peas, sliced radishes and cucumber slices.

In a small bowl combine the dressing ingredients and add to the salad. Mix well and serve at room temperature.

Serves 6.

Cold Chicken and Noodles in a Spicy Sesame Sauce

This sesame sauce is particularly tasty. A delicious meal might include this salad, green beans vinaigrette and buttered French bread rounds crisped in the oven. End the meal with the surprising and satisfying combination of lemon sherbet and hot fudge sauce.

12 ounces linguine

3 chicken breast halves, boned and skinned

1 tablespoon sesame oil

Sauce

1/2 cup sesame paste (either Chinese style or the Middle Eastern tahini)

3 tablespoons water

1 teaspoon Chinese hot oil or more to taste

5 tablespoons soy sauce

3 tablespoons white wine vinegar

1/4 cup salad oil

2 tablespoons minced garlic

*P*oach chicken breasts in seasoned simmering water until just tender, about 15 minutes. Cool and tear or cut meat into thin strips.

*C*ook linguine to al dente stage, drain well and toss with the sesame oil.

*B*lend the sesame paste with the water. Add the rest of the sauce ingredients and mix well.

*C*ombine warm linguine, chicken and sauce. Chill at least four hours. Remove from the refrigerator about 1/2 hour before serving.

*S*erves 6.

Chinese Noodle and Chicken Salad with Peanut Sauce

A visual treat and almost a complete meal on a platter. Add a jellied consomme or hot clear broth for the first course and sliced kiwi and strawberries over ice cream to round out your menu.

8 ounces thin Chinese egg noodles or spaghettini

1 whole chicken breast, at least 1 pound, boned and skinned

1 small onion

1 stalk celery

1 bay leaf

1/2 teaspoon salt

2 cups chicken broth

1 tablespoon salad oil

2 teaspoons sesame oil

Vegetable Garnish

1 cup fresh bean sprouts, blanched and drained

1 cup thinly sliced carrot

1 cup thinly sliced, seeded cucumber

1/2 cup sliced green onions

1 15-ounce can baby corn on the cob, drained and rinsed

Creamy Peanut Sauce

1/2 cup smooth peanut butter

1/3 cup chicken broth

1/4 cup soy sauce

4 tablespoons sesame oil

2 tablespoons minced garlic

2 tablespoons minced fresh gingerroot

2 tablespoons sugar

2 tablespoons red-wine vinegar

1 teaspoon hot chili oil, or more to taste

1/4 cup heavy cream

*C*ook the noodles until al dente, drain, run under cold water and drain again. Cook the chicken breast with the 2 cups broth, salt, onion, celery and bay leaf. Simmer for 15 minutes and cool in the stock; then shred. Reduce the stock, after straining, to about 1/3 cup. Reserve for the sauce.

*O*n a large platter toss the noodles with the chicken, salad oil and 2 teaspoons sesame oil. Garnish with vegetables.

*I*n a food processor fitted with the steel blade or in a blender mix the dressing ingredients, adding the heavy cream after all the other ingredients are well mixed.

*T*ransfer the sauce to a sauceboat and pass with the oriental platter. Serve the salad at room temperature or lightly chilled.

*S*erves 6.

Chinese Noodle and Mushroom Salad with Chicken and Ham

*T*he Chinese mushrooms in this salad are worth tracking down; the larger supermarkets sometimes have them and Oriental markets always do.

12 ounces fine Chinese egg noodles or vermicelli

6 large black Chinese mushrooms (soaked in warm water for 20 minutes)

1/2 chicken breast, poached until tender and shredded

1/2 cup smoked ham, julienned

1/2 tin water chestnuts, rinsed and sliced

1/4 cup sliced green onions

3 tablespoons chopped cilantro (parsley can be substituted)

1 tablespoon salad oil

Dressing

2 tablespoons olive or salad oil

3 tablespoons sesame oil

1 teaspoon hot chili oil (or to taste)

4 tablespoons soy sauce

3 tablespoons cider vinegar

*C*ook the noodles or vermicelli until al dente, drain and toss with 1 tablespoon salad oil.

*D*rain mushrooms, squeeze and pat dry. Discard stems and slice caps.

*C*ombine the dressing ingredients in a small bowl.

*A*dd the mushrooms and remaining ingredients to the noodles, pour the dressing over and toss to coat thoroughly. Taste for seasoning.

*S*erve at room temperature or lightly chilled.

*S*erves 6.

Stir-Fried Chicken, Linguine and Peanuts

_____

_____

_____

_A_nother one-dish meal with Oriental overtones. To make scallion brushes, cut tops off 6 scallions, leaving about 2-3 inches of green. Cut root ends off, then slice white part of scallions in fine strips almost to green part. Place scallions in cold water until ends open and curl slightly.

12 ounces linguine

1 pound boneless and skinless chicken breasts, thinly sliced
(pork loin may also be used)

1 tablespoon cornstarch

1/4 cup vegetable oil

4 scallions, sliced on the diagonal into 1-inch pieces

1 clove garlic, finely minced

4 carrots, peeled and sliced on the diagonal into 1/2 inch pieces and quickly blanched until crisp-tender

2 green peppers, cut into thin strips

1 cup chicken broth, or one chicken bouillon cube in one cup of water

3 tablespoons dry sherry or dry vermouth

3 tablespoons soy sauce

2 tablespoons firmly packed dark brown sugar

1/2 cup peanuts

6 scallion brushes, if desired (see above)

_C_ook linguine to al dente stage, drain well and toss with 1 tablespoon vegetable oil.

_I_n wok or large frying pan, stir-fry green pepper, scallions and garlic in oil for about one minute. Push to one side. Combine chicken (or pork) with cornstarch. Add chicken (or pork) mixture to wok and stir-fry until browned. Add carrots and mix vegetables and meat together; cook about 1 more minute.

_M_ix soy sauce, sherry and brown sugar with chicken broth. Add to mixture and stir over high heat until sauce thickens. Add linguine and toss well. Add peanuts and toss again. Turn into serving bowl and allow flavors to blend.

_S_erve at room temperature. Garnish with scallion brushes if desired.

_S_erves 6.

Hacked Chicken and Noodles in a Spicy Sauce

Once again our favorite sesame sauce that marries so well with chicken and noodles. In this one, you can use creamy peanut butter if Chinese sesame seed paste is not available.

12 ounces vermicelli

1 pound boned chicken breasts, or four chicken breast halves, poached in plain water and shredded

2 cucumbers, peeled, halved, seeded and cut into half rounds

Sauce

1/2 teaspoon ground Szechuan peppercorns

1 inch piece of ginger, minced

2 cloves garlic, minced

2 scallions, minced

5 tablespoons soy sauce

2 tablespoons red wine vinegar

2 teaspoons sugar

2 tablespoons Chinese sesame oil

1 teaspoon hot chili oil

2 tablespoons water

6 tablespoons sesame seed paste (or creamy peanut butter)

Cook pasta until al dente, drain, and toss with 1 tablespoon sesame oil.

Mix all sauce ingredients together. If sauce is too thick, add water; if too thin, add more sesame seed paste.

In large bowl, toss pasta, cucumber, chicken and sauce. Let flavors blend. Serve at room temperature or chilled.

Serves 6.

Oriental Chicken and Pasta with Fruit

*Y*ou might use this salad as a side dish with jumbo shrimp grilled on the hibachi. Frosted bowls of lemon snow topped with candied ginger shreds and coconut make a refreshing dessert.

8 ounces twist pasta

3 cups shredded cooked chicken

8-ounce can pineapple tidbits, drained

1 cup fresh seedless grapes

1 cup thinly sliced celery

1/2 cup thinly sliced water chestnuts

1 recipe Tarragon and Soy Vinaigrette (page 164)

*C*ook pasta until al dente, drain well and toss with 1/4 cup of the Tarragon and Soy Vinaigrette. Chill.

*A*dd chicken, pineapple, grapes, celery and water chestnuts to pasta. Add about 1/2 cup additional dressing and toss lightly. Chill about 1 hour before serving.

*A*dd more dressing before serving if necessary.

*S*erves 6.

Sesame Chicken and Twists Salad

A *whole new taste treat. Sesame seed, not sesame oil, is used here. The effect is entirely different.*

8 ounces pasta twists

4 chicken breast halves, poached, skinned, and meat cut into 1/4 inch strips

1 box frozen snow peas, thawed only

1 can water chestnuts, sliced

1 bunch scallions, sliced diagonally

1/2 cup sesame seeds, lightly toasted

Salt and pepper to taste

Dressing

4 tablespoons dry sherry

1 egg yolk

3 tablespoons lemon juice

2 tablespoons Dijon-style mustard

2 tablespoons soy sauce

2 tablespoons sugar

1 teaspoon minced fresh ginger or 1/2 teaspoon ground

1/2 cup olive oil

1/2 cup vegetable oil

Hot pepper sauce or red pepper flakes to taste

*C*ook pasta to al dente stage, drain well, and toss with 1 tablespoon vegetable oil to prevent sticking.

*I*n large bowl, gently but thoroughly toss pasta, chicken, snow peas, scallions, water chestnuts, sesame seeds. Add salt and pepper to taste.

*T*o make dressing, mix well all dressing ingredients except oil and hot pepper. Gradually add oil to dressing, beating constantly until mixture is emulsified. Add hot pepper sauce or pepper flakes to taste.

*P*our dressing over chicken and pasta mixture and toss well.

*S*erve chilled or at room temperature.

*S*erves 6.

Fettuccine and Chicken Nicoise Salad

This salad is a popular specialty of La Prima carry-outs in Houston, Dallas and Washington, D.C.

12 ounces fettuccine

1 pound poached chicken breast, shredded or sliced into thin strips

3 medium tomatoes, diced

4 tablespoons capers, rinsed and drained

3/4 cup mayonnaise

2 tablespoons chopped fresh dill

1 teaspoon salt

1 teaspoon freshly ground black pepper

Mix together chicken, tomatoes, mayonnaise, dill and salt and pepper. Refrigerate several hours.

Cook pasta until al dente, drain, rinse with cold water and drain again. Mix pasta and chicken salad and refrigerate until well chilled.

Serves 6.

Chicken, Green Pepper and Linguine, Oriental Style

---

*T*his dish is good hot or warm, but we think it's best served chilled on large white plates with chopsticks.

12 ounces linguine

1 pound chicken breasts, boned and skinned and cut into thin strips

4 large green peppers, cut into thin strips

1 bunch scallions, cut on the diagonal into 1 inch pieces

2-3 hot dried red peppers

1 teaspoon Szechuan peppercorns

2 tablespoons cornstarch

Dressing

6 tablespoons soy sauce

2 teaspoons sesame oil

2 tablespoons vinegar

2 tablespoons dry sherry or vermouth

*C*ook linguine until al dente, drain well, toss with 1 tablespoon vegetable oil. Depending on how you plan to serve the salad, keep hot or let come to room temperature.

*H*eat 2 tablespoons vegetable oil in wok or large skillet until quite hot. Stir-fry vegetables with 2-3 hot dried peppers and peppercorns over high heat; push to one side or remove from pan.

*S*hake chicken strips with cornstarch in bag; stir-fry 2-3 minutes or until lightly browned.

*M*ix vegetables and chicken together.

*M*ix dressing ingredients together; pour over chicken and vegetables; stir-fry about 1 minute.

*A*dd linguine, blend well. Serve at desired temperature.

*S*erves 6.

Chicken and Noodles in a Chinese Chili Paste Sauce

Intensely flavored Chinese chili paste with garlic adds a special zip to this salad.

12 ounces linguine or thin spaghetti

4 chicken breast halves

1 medium onion stuck with 3 whole cloves

1 stalk celery, halved

3 cloves garlic, minced

1 tablespoon chopped fresh ginger

1 tablespoon dry sherry

4 tablespoons cold tea

4 tablespoons soy sauce

1-1/2 teaspoons chili paste with garlic (available at Chinese groceries and gourmet shops)

2 teaspoons cornstarch

1 bunch scallions, sliced on the diagonal into 1 inch pieces

Salad oil

Cook pasta to al dente stage, drain well, and toss with 1 tablespoon salad oil.

Poach chicken in water to cover, with onion and celery, for 20 minutes. Remove chicken and reserve broth.

Cut or tear chicken into thin strips and add to pasta.

In wok or skillet, briefly saute scallions, garlic and ginger in 1-2 tablespoons oil. Add sherry, cold tea, soy sauce, chili paste, cornstarch and ½ cup reserved broth. Cook over high heat about 1 minute.

Pour over pasta and chicken and toss well. Add by the spoonful more broth as necessary. Allow flavors to blend at least 2 hours before serving. Serve at room temperature or chilled.

Serves 6.

Layered Chicken and Pasta Salad

A make-in-advance main dish that is nutritious as well as attractive. Serve in a clear glass bowl so that family or guests can enjoy the colorful layering.

1-1/2 cups macaroni or other tube pasta

3 cups cubed cooked chicken

1-1/2 teaspoons curry powder

1/2 teaspoon salt

1/4 teaspoon paprika

1/4 teaspoon freshly ground pepper

2 cups shredded iceberg lettuce

2 cups shredded romaine lettuce

1 large cucumber, peeled, seeded and sliced

1 large green pepper, chopped . . . red pepper looks smashing if available

4 green onions, chopped

Dressing

1-1/2 cups good mayonnaise

1 tablespoon milk

2 tablespoons lemon juice

1 teaspoon salt

1/4 teaspoon freshly ground pepper

2 tablespoons chopped parsley and 2 tomatoes, cut in wedges, for garnish

*C*ook pasta until al dente, drain well. Stir in 1 tablespoon oil to prevent sticking.

*I*n medium bowl mix chicken with curry powder, salt, paprika and pepper.

*I*n a large clear bowl (about 4 quart size) layer iceberg and romaine lettuce, curried chicken, cucumber, macaroni and green pepper.

*S*tir together mayonnaise, milk, lemon juice, salt and pepper.

*S*pread on top of layered ingredients. Cover tightly with plastic wrap and chill several hours or overnight.

*G*arnish with parsley and tomato wedges before serving. Toss at the table.

*S*erves 6.

Dilled Chicken and Linguine Salad

An excellent luncheon entree, served with sliced tomatoes and warm rolls. Kids will love this salad too.

12 ounces linguine or fettuccine

1 whole chicken breast, boned and skinned

4 medium dill pickles, chopped

4 stalks of celery, thinly sliced

6 green onions, chopped

2 tablespoons capers, rinsed and drained

12 small pimiento-stuffed olives

2 hard-cooked eggs, chopped

Dressing

1/2 cup sour cream

1/2 cup mayonnaise

Juice of 1 lemon

1/2 teaspoon dried dillweed or 2 teaspoons fresh dill, chopped

1 teaspoon salt

1/2 teaspoon freshly ground pepper

*B*arely cover the chicken breast with water and add 1 teaspoon salt, 1 small onion, 2 whole cloves and 4 peppercorns. Simmer 15 minutes. Remove from broth and cool. Shred meat coarsely.

*W*hile chicken is simmering, cook pasta until al dente, drain and toss with 1 tablespoon salad oil. Set aside to cool to room temperature.

*M*ix dressing ingredients together in a small bowl. Gently mix the pasta, chicken, pickles, celery, onions and capers and about 2/3 of the dressing. Add more dressing as needed. Refrigerate if not serving immediately. Mound the mixture on a lettuce-lined platter and garnish with the chopped eggs and olives.

*S*erves 6.

Green Noodles with Proscuitto and Chicken

_____
_____
_____

A *lovely contrast of colors as well as taste. Add the sliced mushrooms just before serving for extra freshness. If prosciutto is not available, use crisp fried bacon.*

12 ounces green fettuccine

2 chicken breast halves, boned and skinned

1/4 pound prosciutto, or 1/2 pound bacon crisply fried

1 cup coarsely chopped seeded tomatoes

1/2 cup chopped green onion tops

1/4 pound mushrooms, sliced

1/4 cup chopped parsley

Fresh basil leaves or oregano for garnish

Dressing

1/2 cup sour cream

1/4 cup mayonnaise

1/4 cup olive oil

1 teaspoon Italian seasonings

1/2 teaspoon salt

1/4 teaspoon freshly ground pepper

Cook fettuccine until al dente, drain well and toss with 2 tablespoons vegetable oil; cool.

Poach chicken breasts in seasoned, simmering water until just done, about 15 minutes; cool.

Dice the chicken and the prosciutto (or crumble the crisp bacon) and add to the pasta.

Mix the dressing ingredients and add to the pasta along with the chopped tomatoes and onion tops. Refrigerate until serving time.

Sprinkle the sliced mushrooms and fresh herbs on top just before serving and toss at the table.

Serves 6.

Rotelle and Chicken Salad

_A_ny type of cooked left-over chicken, even from Sunday's barbecue, is suitable for this melange of red, white and green salad ingredients.

12 ounces rotelle

2 cups shredded or cubed cooked chicken

2 cups broccoli florets

1 large green or red sweet pepper, thinly sliced

1/2 box cherry tomatoes, halved if large

1/2 cup sliced mushrooms

1/4 cup toasted slivered almonds or
2 tablespoons toasted sunflower seeds

1/2 cup Low-Calorie Creamy Dressing
(page 173) or 1/2 cup Herbed
Vinaigrette (page 161)

1/4 cup chopped parsley

Cook pasta until al dente, drain thoroughly and toss with 1 tablespoon vegetable oil.

Plunge broccoli florets into pan of boiling water for 1 minute, then rinse with cold water and drain thoroughly. Add chicken, vegetables and nuts to pasta with dressing of your choice. Mix thoroughly and taste for salt and pepper. Sprinkle with chopped parsley and serve at room temperature or lightly chilled.

Serves 6.

Chicken and Snow Peas with Fruit and Pasta

*S*erve this refreshing and unusual combination on a torrid summer evening to your weekend guests.

8 ounces spaghetti or fusilli

1 whole chicken breast, boned and skinned

2 tablespoons butter

1/4 cup olive oil

Salt and pepper to taste

5 or 6 nectarines, depending on size, pitted and sliced

4 red plums, pitted and sliced

1/4 pound snow peas or sugar snap peas, or 10-ounce box frozen snow peas, thawed

6 green onions, sliced

1 cup walnuts, coarsely chopped

Dressing

1/4 cup walnut oil

1/4 cup salad oil

1/4 cup white wine vinegar

1 tablespoon crumbled fresh rosemary or 1 teaspoon dried rosemary

1 teaspoon salt or more to taste

1/2 teaspoon freshly ground black pepper

*M*ix dressing before preparing other ingredients. Set aside; do not refrigerate.

*C*ook pasta until al dente, drain, rinse with cold water and drain again. Toss with 1/4 cup dressing. Do not refrigerate.

*M*elt butter in olive oil; saute chicken breast in the oil mixture until just done; do not brown. Cool, slice into thin strips.

*P*our boiling water over pea pods; do not cook.

*C*ombine chicken, nectarines, plums, snow peas or sugar snap peas, onions and walnuts. Toss gently with remaining dressing. Chill.

*A*t serving time add chicken mixture to pasta and toss thoroughly but gently.

Serves 6.

Hot Chicken and Pasta Salad

An all-in-one meal that combines hot and cold, meat and vegetables. Use a wok if you have one, or a large frying pan. Because wok cookery is so quick, be sure to have everything sliced and ready to go before you heat the oil.

8 ounces twists

1 pound boneless chicken breasts, skinned and cubed

1/4 cup cornstarch

1/4 cup vegetable oil

2 cloves of garlic, flattened slightly with flat blade of knife

1/2 box cherry tomatoes, halved

1 can water chestnuts, drained and cut in thin slices

1/4 pound fresh mushrooms, cleaned and cut in thin slices

2 scallions, thinly sliced and including some green

1 cup celery, thinly sliced

1/2 cup soy sauce

2 cups finely shredded iceberg lettuce

Cook twists to al dente stage, drain well and toss with 1 tablespoon vegetable oil.

In brown paper bag, shake cornstarch and chicken together until well coated. Saute garlic cloves in vegetable oil until lightly browned; discard garlic. Quickly saute chicken cubes in the flavored oil until browned. Remove. Add water chestnuts, mushrooms, scallions and celery and saute over high heat until crisp-tender (2-3 minutes). Add chicken, twists, and the soy sauce to pan; blend well.

In serving bowl, toss chicken and pasta mixture with the halved tomatoes and the lettuce. Serve immediately.

Serves 6.

Vermicelli and Chicken Salad with Lemon Dressing

_____

_____

_____

*T*angy but light with a Far East appeal.

8 ounces vermicelli

3 chicken breast halves or 1-1/2 pounds chicken pieces

1 small onion stuck with 3 whole cloves

1 carrot, sliced

1 stalk celery, with leaves

1 clove garlic

2 teaspoons salt

6 peppercorns

2 cups fresh bean sprouts, rinsed in boiling water and drained

1 cup bamboo shoots, julienned

Dressing

3/4 cup broth from the chicken

1 tablespoon sugar

1 tablespoon soy sauce

1/2 cup lemon juice

1 teaspoon cornstarch

2 teaspoons cold water

1 teaspoon grated lemon rind

White pepper to taste

Garnish

3 green onions, cut into 1 inch pieces, then slivered vertically

2 lemons, halved, seeded and very thinly sliced

*C*ombine the chicken with water to cover, onion, carrot, celery, garlic clove, salt and peppercorns. Bring to a boil, reduce heat, and simmer until just tender.

*R*emove chicken and cool. Strain broth and reserve.

*C*ook vermicelli until al dente, drain, run under cold water and drain again.

*S*kin and bone chicken and shred coarsely.

*M*ix the cornstarch with the cold water and add to the dressing ingredients in a small sauce pan. Simmer until slightly thickened; set aside to cool.

*I*n a large shallow bowl toss the vermicelli, chicken, bean sprouts, bamboo shoots and dressing. Sprinkle slivered green onions on top and surround with the lemon slices.

*S*erves 6.

Orzo and Poultry Salad

*D*elicate rice-shaped pasta teams up with yesterday's left-over chicken or turkey—or even shreds of ham. For a winter treat, substitute anise-flavored fennel for sliced celery.

1-1/2 cups orzo

2 cups shredded cooked chicken, turkey or ham

1 cup chopped green onions (use tops and bottoms)

1 cup sliced celery or the stem part of a fennel bulb

1/4 cup chopped parsley

Dressing

3/4 cup mayonnaise

1 teaspoon salt

1/2 teaspoon pepper

2 tablespoons tarragon vinegar

1/2 teaspoon crumbled dry tarragon

*C*ook pasta until al dente, drain, rinse with cold water and drain again.

*B*lend dressing ingredients in a serving bowl. Add the pasta and remaining ingredients and toss gently but thoroughly. Taste for seasonings and chill until serving time.

*S*erves 6.

Creamy and Curried Chicken, Apple and Fusilli Salad

_S_erve this main-course curried salad with a zesty chutney and some _interesting Indian breads such as puri or chappati._

12 ounces fusilli	_Dressing_
1 whole chicken breast	1 cup mayonnaise
3 medium red apples, unpeeled and diced	1/4 cup light cream
1/2 cup raisins	2 teaspoons curry powder, or more to taste
1 cup chopped celery	1-1/2 teaspoons salt
1/2 cup sliced ripe olives	1/8 teaspoon cayenne
1/2 cup green onion tops only, sliced 1 inch long	1 tablespoon lemon juice
1/4 cup slivered almonds	

_C_ook pasta until al dente, drain, rinse with cold water and drain again.

_P_oach chicken breast with a small onion stuck with 2 whole cloves, 4 peppercorns, a small stalk of celery and 1 teaspoon salt. Simmer gently just until firm to the touch. Cool and shred. (Save broth for a cold soup base.) Cover chicken with plastic wrap and refrigerate.

_B_lend dressing ingredients in a small bowl.

_A_dd the chicken, apples, raisins, celery, olives, green onions and almonds to the pasta. Pour about half the dressing over the pasta mixture and toss lightly but well.

_C_over and refrigerate at least one hour. Mix with the remaining dressing before serving.

_S_erves 6.

Mostaccioli, Turkey and Vegetable Salad

A *tasty way to use up leftover bird. This main course salad is relatively low in calories, so splurge with a luscious dessert.*

12 ounces mostaccioli

3 cups leftover turkey, cubed

1 box frozen peas, briefly cooked and drained

1 box frozen French-style (julienned) green beans, briefly cooked and drained

1/2 cup coarsely chopped radishes

4 scallions, sliced into small rounds and including some green

1 cup Basic Vinaigrette
(page 160)

*C*ook pasta to al dente stage, drain, rinse with cold water, and drain again.

*T*oss with the turkey and the vegetables. Add the vinaigrette by the spoonful, tossing well after each addition; you may not need the entire cup. Adjust seasonings.

*C*over and chill at least four hours to let flavors blend.

*S*erves 6.

Turkey with Ginger and Linguine

---

*T*urn *left-over holiday turkey into an oriental surprise. To start, serve won-ton soup from your local Chinese carry-out. For fun, end with fortune cookies.*

8 ounces linguine or tagliatelle pasta

2 cups turkey meat cut into strips

2 cups cooked peas (fresh or frozen)

1/2 cup chopped green onions

1/2 cup slivered or sliced almonds, toasted

1/4 cup chopped red pepper or 3 table-spoons chopped pimiento

Dressing

3/4 cup oil, half salad and half olive

1/3 cup tarragon vinegar

3 tablespoons Dijon mustard

2 teaspoons freshly grated ginger

1 teaspoon salt

1/4 teaspoon freshly grated pepper

*C*ook pasta until al dente, drain, rinse with cold water and drain again. Place in a large serving bowl.

*I*n a medium bowl mix the dressing ingredients. Add 1/4 cup to the pasta and toss gently.

*T*o the remaining dressing add the turkey, peas, onions, almonds and red pepper or pimiento. Mix thoroughly but carefully. Put on top of the pasta and refrigerate until 1/2 hour before serving.

*T*oss at the table.

*S*erves 6.

Turkey and Asparagus Pasta Salad

Left-over turkey will rise to new heights with this palate- and eye-pleasing salad.

12 ounces bow tie or farfalle pasta	*Dressing*
24 small, very thin slices of turkey	1 cup plain yogurt or sour cream
1 pound asparagus	1/2 cup ricotta cheese
4 tomatoes, peeled and thinly sliced	2 tablespoons basil or white wine vinegar
1/2 bunch watercress, coarse stems removed	1 clove garlic, minced
	10 fresh basil leaves, coarsely chopped
2 tablespoons olive oil	1 tablespoon finely chopped celery leaves
	1/2 teaspoon sugar
	1 teaspoon salt
	1/4 teaspoon freshly ground pepper

*C*ook pasta until al dente, drain, rinse under cold water and drain again. Mix with 2 tablespoons olive oil and refrigerate.

*W*ash asparagus, break off woody ends and peel if you wish; cut into 1-inch lengths.

*T*ear watercress into bite-size pieces.

*C*ombine the sliced turkey, tomatoes, asparagus and watercress. Refrigerate until serving time.

*T*horoughly mix the dressing but do not make it smooth. Taste for seasonings.

*A*t serving time toss the pasta with about 1/2 cup dressing and arrange in a shallow bowl or deep platter. Arrange the turkey mixture on top and drizzle the remaining dressing over all.

*S*erves 6.

Main Course Pasta "Club" Salad

---

*T*his main course salad uses everyone's favorite club sandwich ingredients to provide a refreshing alternative to the usual sandwich-type meal. Round out the menu with a green vegetable, cooked crisp-tender, a chilled white wine and chocolate cake for dessert.

12 ounces rotini

2 cups cooked chicken or turkey, cubed

8 ounces bacon, crisply cooked and crumbled

2 ripe tomatoes, cut in small pieces, or 1/2 box cherry tomatoes, cut in half if large

2 cups iceberg lettuce, cut in 1/4 inch slices

1/2 cup julienned Swiss cheese

Salt and freshly ground pepper to taste

Dressing

1 cup mayonnaise

2 tablespoons white wine vinegar

2 tablespoons lemon juice

*C*ook rotini until al dente, drain, rinse under cold water and drain again. (Toss with 2 tablespoons oil if not mixing right away with the other ingredients.)

*B*lend dressing ingredients until smooth. Mix dressing, rotini, chicken and bacon together, and refrigerate at least 1 hour so flavors can blend.
Just before serving, toss with the tomatoes, lettuce and Swiss cheese.
Add salt and freshly ground black pepper to taste.

*S*erves 6.

Turkey Tetrazzini Salad Norwood

We've given an old standby a new twist. The recipe can easily be doubled or tripled for a buffet supper or a Little League picnic.

12 ounces linguine, broken into thirds	*Dressing*
2 cups cooked turkey, cubed	1 cup cottage cheese
1/2 pound fresh mushrooms	1/4 cup milk
1 box frozen tiny peas, thawed only	2 tablespoons lemon juice
1 small jar diced pimientos	2 tablespoons Worcestershire sauce
1/2 cup slivered almonds	1/2 teaspoon thyme
Salt and freshly ground pepper to taste	Tabasco sauce to taste

Cook linguine until al dente, drain, rinse under cold water and drain again.

Toss with 2 tablespoons oil to prevent sticking.

Clean and thinly slice mushrooms. Drain pimientos. Saute almonds in a little olive oil or butter until lightly browned; drain on paper towels and reserve.

Whirl first five dressing ingredients in a blender or food processor until smooth. Add Tabasco drop by drop to taste; dressing should have a little zip to it.

Combine linguine, turkey, mushrooms, peas, pimientos in a large bowl. Add dressing as necessary—you may not need all of it. Toss well and refrigerate at least 1 hour. Just before serving, toss with the reserved almonds and add salt and pepper to taste.

Serves 6.

Pasta Salads with Meat

Pasta Salads with Meat

---

*B*its of yesterday's dinner roast, not enough to make a meal alone, can be combined with pasta, vegetables and seasonings for a delectable new dish that no one would ever guess got its start as leftovers. In fact, you may want to cook a little extra meat tonight with tomorrow night's pasta salad dinner in mind.

Pepperoni and Shell Salad Bloch

*I*talian bread and an attractive platter of assorted cheeses and fruit are all you need to serve with this salad for a luncheon or light supper for family or friends.

8 ounces small shell pasta

1 14-ounce can artichoke hearts

3 bell peppers, preferably red but green are fine

1/2 pound broccoli florets

1/2 pound pepperoni sausage

3 tablespoons diced pimientos

2 tablespoons chopped Italian or regular parsley

Dressing

1 cup mayonnaise

1/4 cup red wine vinegar

1/2 teaspoon salt

1/2 teaspoon freshly ground pepper

2 teaspoons coarsely chopped fresh basil or 1 teaspoon dried basil

1 teaspoon oregano

1 tablespoon chopped Italian or regular parsley

*C*ook pasta until al dente, drain, rinse under cold water and drain again. Toss with 1 tablespoon olive oil.

*D*rain and quarter artichoke hearts.

*S*eed and thinly slice peppers.

*S*team broccoli florets for 3 minutes and run under cold water; drain well.

*T*hinly slice pepperoni sausage.

*T*oss all the above ingredients with the dressing, adjust seasonings. Serve chilled.

*S*erves 6.

Pasta Deli Salad

*W*hat could be simpler than one stop at the deli counter, then cooking up a pot of pasta?

8 ounces twist, shell, or penne

1/4 pound hard salami, cut into thin strips

1/4 pound provolone cheese, cut into thin strips

1 small red onion, cut into thin rings

1 cup chopped green or red pepper (or try sliced pimientos for a change)

1 cup black olives, sliced

1/4 cup chopped parsley

Dressing

1/2 cup salad oil

3 tablespoons red wine vinegar

1 teaspoon Dijon-style mustard

1/2 teaspoon oregano, crushed

1/2 teaspoon celery seed

1/2 teaspoon salt

Freshly ground pepper to taste

1/4 cup grated parmesan cheese

*M*ix all dressing ingredients thoroughly in a medium size bowl.

*C*ook pasta until al dente, drain. Toss in a large bowl with 1/4 cup dressing. Do not refrigerate.

*A*dd salami, cheese, onion, pepper, olives and parsley to remaining dressing, toss well.

*C*ombine the deli ingredients with the pasta and toss together. Serve at room temperature or lightly chilled if the day is hot.

*S*erves 6.

Antipasto Salad Platter

This colorful salad is the perfect way to begin an Italian-style meal. The main course might be a crispy chicken roasted with lemon: Slice one lemon, add to chicken cavity; rub bird with olive oil and salt and pepper; roast at 400 degrees until well browned. Make a sauce of the pan juices, juice from the lemon slices, and a little white wine and/or chicken broth; cook down until syrupy. Makes about 1 tablespoon sauce for each serving of chicken. Serve with Italian bread and a light red wine.

8 ounces small shells or other small pasta

2 green and/or red sweet peppers, diced

1/2 pound fresh mushrooms, washed and sliced

1/4 pound provolone cheese, cubed

1 20-ounce can chick peas, rinsed and drained

1/4 pound salami, cut in strips

1/4 pound black Greek olives, pitted

2 tablespoons chopped parsley

1 tin anchovy fillets, drained

Dressing

1/2 cup olive or salad oil

1/4 cup fresh lemon juice

1 teaspoon salt

1/4 teaspoon pepper

1/8 teaspoon red pepper flakes, or Tabasco to taste

1 clove garlic, crushed

1 teaspoon dried basil leaves, or 1 tablespoon fresh basil, chopped

Cook pasta until al dente, drain well, and toss with 1 tablespoon salad oil. In a small bowl thoroughly blend dressing ingredients; adjust seasonings as necessary. In large bowl, toss pasta with the dressing. Cool.

Add rest of ingredients to pasta mixture; toss lightly. Refrigerate, covered, for one hour. Toss well before serving.

Serves 6.

Colorful Vegetables and Pasta with Pancetta

T his salad is always a knockout on buffet tables. Pancetta is similar to bacon but cured, not smoked, and is round and tightly packed like salami. Worth looking for at the Italian grocery. A non-fatty salami can be substituted.

8 ounces dried gnocchi or cavatelli, half plain and half tomato flavored if possible (this is more for color than taste)

1 cup broccoli florets

1/2 cup cauliflower florets

1 cup quartered mushrooms

1/2 cup green onion, cut into 1/2 inch pieces

1/2 cup sliced pitted ripe olives

1/4 pound pancetta, sliced 1/4 inch thick and julienned

1 avocado, peeled and sliced

1 large, ripe tomato, seeded and chopped, or 12 cherry tomatoes, left whole if small

1 recipe Herbed Vinaigrette (page 161)

*C*ook pasta until al dente, drain, rinse with cold water and drain again. Toss with 1 tablespoon olive oil.

*B*lanch broccoli for 1 minute in boiling water, drain, rinse with cold water and drain again. Add to pasta and toss lightly. Cover with plastic wrap and chill. Add cauliflower, mushrooms, green onions and olives to 1/2 cup of the Herbed Vinaigrette dressing and marinate until serving time or at least 1 hour, covered and refrigerated.

*J*ust before serving add pancetta and marinated vegetables to the pasta and broccoli. Toss gently. Taste for seasoning and adjust if necessary.

*A*dd avocado, tomato and remaining dressing and toss again, very gently. Serve lightly chilled.

*S*erves 6.

Salami, Garbanzo Beans and Penne a la Tuscany

This variation of the better known Tuna, Bean and Pasta Salad makes a wonderful luncheon dish or addition to an antipasto platter.

8 ounces penne or other short tube pasta

1 pound hard salami, not sliced

1 16-ounce can garbanzo beans (chickpeas)

1 medium red onion, thinly sliced

1/4 cup capers, rinsed and drained

1 cup chopped parsely, preferably the flat-leaved type

1 cup jumbo ripe olives, with pits

Dressing

1/2 cup olive oil

1/4 cup red wine vinegar

3 cloves garlic, minced

1 teaspoon salt

1/2 teaspoon freshly ground black pepper

1/2 teaspoon thyme

Whisk dressing ingredients in a small bowl. Set aside.

Cook pasta until al dente, drain and transfer to a serving bowl. Toss with 1/4 cup dressing.

Slice salami thickly, then julienne. Add to pasta with beans, onion, capers, parsley and olives. Add remaining dressing and toss again. Do not chill; serve at room temperature.

Serves 6.

Rotelle, Ham and Fontina Cheese Salad Lewis

A *hearty, well-balanced and year-round main course. In the winter start with a hot, light soup and accompany the salad with Tomatoes Provencale (in 350-degree preheated oven bake cherry tomatoes sprinkled with oil, garlic and rosemary for 10 minutes) and crisp French bread.*

8 ounces rotelle or other twist pasta

1 pound ham (leftover is best), julienned, about two cups

1/2 pound fontina or Swiss cheese, coarsely grated, about 2 cups

2 cups red cabbage, finely shredded

1/2 cup coarsely chopped walnuts, toasted

Dressing

1/4 cup white wine

3 tablespoons white wine vinegar

3 tablespoons chopped green onions

1 clove garlic, minced

1-1/2 tablespoons Dijon mustard

3/4 teaspoon salt

1/4 teaspoon freshly ground pepper

2/3 cup olive oil, or half olive and half salad

1/4 cup minced parsley

*C*ook pasta until al dente, drain, rinse with cold water, and drain again. Mix dressing ingredients. In a large bowl, toss pasta with 2/3 cup of the dressing. Cover and cool to room temperature.

*M*ix the ham and cheese with half the remaining dressing and chill.

*T*oss the shredded cabbage with the remaining dressing and chill.

*S*hortly before serving, toss together the pasta and the ham, cheese and cabbage mixtures. Sprinkle with the chopped walnuts and serve.

*S*erves 6.

Vermicelli with Asparagus and Ham

*W*hat a nice way to celebrate the first asparagus of spring and enjoy
leftover Easter ham. A platter of tangy deviled eggs from the Easter egg
hunt complete a lunch for holiday visitors.

12 ounces vermicelli

1/2 pound fresh asparagus, ends broken
off and cut into 1 inch pieces

1 small onion, halved and sliced

1-1/2 cups ham slivers

1/4 cup olive oil, divided

2 tablespoons water

1 teaspoon salt, divided

1/2 teaspoon freshly ground pepper

1/2 teaspoon marjoram, crushed

3 tablespoons chopped parsley

*C*ook vermicelli until al dente, drain and toss with 1 tablespoon oil.

*H*eat 1 tablespoon oil in skillet; add asparagus, onions, 1/2 teaspoon
salt and marjoram and toss to coat. Add water and stir-fry until tender
but crisp.

*A*dd vegetables, ham, remaining oil, ground pepper and parsley to pasta
and toss gently. Taste and adjust seasonings.

*S*erve at room temperature.

*S*erves 6.

Pasta and Ham Layered Salad

Prepare this contrast of color and taste in advance to accommodate a busy schedule.

1-1/2 cups shell macaroni

2 cups shredded iceberg lettuce

2 cups ham or 1 cup ham and 1 cup hard salami, cut into julienne strips

3 hard-cooked eggs, sliced

1 10-ounce package frozen tiny green peas, thawed

1 cup shredded Monterey Jack cheese

Dressing

1 cup mayonnaise

1/4 cup sour cream

2 teaspoons Dijon mustard

1/4 cup chopped green onion

1 teaspoon salt

1/2 teaspoon freshly ground pepper

2 tablespoons chopped parsley, for garnish

Cook macaroni until al dente, drain, rinse with cold water and drain again. Mix with 1 tablespoon salad oil and set aside to cool.

Combine the mayonnaise, sour cream, mustard, green onion, salt and ground pepper. Set aside.

In a 3-quart bowl, preferably glass, layer the lettuce and top with the cooled macaroni. Next layer the egg slices and sprinkle with salt and pepper. Add in layers the ham (or ham and salami), thawed peas and shredded cheese. Spread the dressing mixture carefully over the top and to the edge of the bowl. Cover with plastic wrap and refrigerate at least overnight. Sprinkle with chopped parsley before serving. Toss at the table.

Serves 6.

Pasta and Ham Picnic Salad

*F*or a casual look and an easy cleanup, serve this old-fashioned picnic salad in a foil-lined basket. Remember to keep salad well chilled until serving time.

8 ounces rigatoni or elbow macaroni

1 pound cooked ham steak, julienned into 1-1/2 inch lengths

2 red or green sweet peppers, diced

1 large red onion, diced

10 small sweet pickles, sliced

1/2 basket cherry tomatoes, halved

2 hard-cooked eggs, chopped

2 tablespoons chopped fresh dill

Dressing

1 cup mayonnaise

1/4 cup sour cream

2 teaspoons dry au jus gravy mix (powdered bouillon can be substituted)

2 tablespoons pickle juice

1 tablespoon vinegar

1/2 teaspoon salt

1/4 teaspoon pepper

1-2 garlic cloves, minced

*C*ook pasta until al dente, drain, rinse with cold water and drain thoroughly. Chill in large bowl.

*M*ix well all dressing ingredients.

*A*dd ham, peppers, onion, pickles, tomatoes and eggs to pasta. Add dressing and mix thoroughly. Sprinkle chopped dill on top and refrigerate until serving time. Toss before serving.

*S*erves 6.

Rotelle with Beef and Mushrooms

This is especially nice when the steak is grilled to medium rare on the outdoor grill and home-grown tomatoes are at their peak.

8 ounces rotelle or other twist-type pasta

1 small flank steak (about 2 cups steak), grilled and thinly sliced

1/2 pound fresh mushrooms, thinly sliced

3 dill pickles, thinly sliced

2 tomatoes, cut into thin wedges for garnish

2 eggs, hard cooked and coarsely chopped

Dressing

1/2 cup olive oil or half olive and half salad

3 tablespoons white wine vinegar

2 tablespoons capers, rinsed, drained and minced

2 teaspoons Dijon mustard

2 tablespoons minced fresh parsley

1/2 teaspoon dried tarragon or 1 table-spoon fresh

1/2 teaspoon salt or more to taste

1/4 teaspoon freshly ground pepper

*M*ix dressing ingredients thoroughly and pour over the prepared sliced meat and mushrooms. Marinate about two hours, refrigerated.

*M*eanwhile, cook the pasta until al dente, drain, rinse under cold water and drain again. Turn into a large bowl and toss with 2 tablespoons salad oil. Cool to room temperature.

*P*repare pickles, tomatoes and eggs. Shortly before serving, add the marinated meat and mushrooms and the pickles to the pasta and toss well. Garnish with tomato wedges and sprinkle with the chopped eggs.

Serves 6.

Beef, Snow Peas and Bow Tie Pasta with Bleu Cheese Dressing

A casual Sunday night supper might include this satisfying salad. During the summer try cold grilled beef with fresh sugar snap peas. In a hurry? Use deli roast beef and frozen snow peas.

8 ounces bow tie (farfalle) pasta

1 pound rare roast beef, cut into short thin slices

1/2 pound mushrooms, thinly sliced

1/4 pound snow peas or 1 box frozen snow peas, thawed only

1/2 bunch watercress, heavy stems removed

Dressing

1 cup sour cream

1/2 cup bleu cheese, crumbled

1/4 cup light cream

4 tablespoons red wine vinegar

2 green onions, finely chopped

1/2 teaspoon salt

1/4 teaspoon freshly ground pepper

Cook pasta until al dente, drain, rinse with cold water and drain again. Toss with 1 to 2 tablespoons oil to prevent sticking. Cool to room temperature.

Drop fresh snow peas or sugar snap peas into boiling salted water and cook 1 minute. Drain and run under cold water. Cut in half and chill.

Mix dressing ingredients in blender or food processor until just blended but not smooth. Cover and chill.

In a large shallow bowl or platter arrange the pasta and spoon some dressing over it. Starting at the outer edge of the platter, make a ring of watercress on top of the pasta, then mushrooms and snow peas; mound the beef in the center. Drizzle each ring with dressing and pass the remaining dressing at the table.

Serve chilled.

Serves 6.

Piquant Beef, Cherry Tomato and Pasta Salad

S*ave some of last night's roast beef or grill a small steak for this satisfying salad. Precede the salad with a cold cream of carrot or zucchini soup—or a hot soup if there's a nip in the air.*

8 ounces rotelle or shell macaroni

3 cups cubed left-over roast beef or steak, preferably rare

18 cherry tomatoes, halved if large

1 cup chopped green onions

1/3 cup chopped parsley

1/2 cup rinsed and drained capers

10 or 12 leaves fresh basil, torn, or 2 teaspoons dried basil, crushed

1/2 cup Italian or Greek cured black olives

Dressing

1 cup salad oil, or half salad and half olive oil

1/2 cup white wine or herb vinegar

2-ounce tin anchovy fillets, including oil

3 cloves garlic, chopped

1-1/2 teaspoons salt

1/2 teaspoon freshly ground black pepper

1 teaspoon sugar

Cook pasta until al dente, drain, rinse under cold water and drain again. Transfer to a large bowl and toss with 1 tablespoon of the oil.

If you are using a food processor, add to it all the dressing ingredients and combine until well mixed. Or, mash the anchovy fillets with a fork, then add the other dressing ingredients and whisk together until well blended.

To the pasta add the cubed beef, green onions, parsley, capers and basil and toss thoroughly. Add the tomatoes and olives and the dressing and toss again, gently.

Serves 6.

Beef and Pasta with Broccoli and Asparagus

This salad is a natural when asparagus is at its peak—and its cheapest. What a treat, though, to serve in mid-winter when some California spears manage to slip into the supermarkets. Start with a hot soup, accompany with hot rolls and you won't notice the cold outside.

8 ounces fettuccine, or bucatini if available

1 small flank steak, or about 2 cups cut into strips

1 bunch broccoli, about 1-1/2 pounds

1 pound fresh asparagus

Dressing

1/2 cup soy sauce

1/2 cup salad oil

3 tablespoons sesame oil

1-1/2 inch piece fresh ginger, peeled and grated

2 cloves garlic, minced

1/2 teaspoon freshly ground pepper, or to taste

1 teaspoon sugar

1 tablespoon minced onion

*B*roil flank steak to medium rare or quickly pan-fry. Cool and thinly slice.

*C*ook pasta until al dente, drain, rinse under cold water and drain thoroughly. Toss with 2 tablespoons of the 1/2 cup of salad oil.

*R*emove the stalks from the broccoli and save for another use. Break the florets into bite-size pieces. Break off the woody ends of the asparagus and wash well; peel stalks if you wish.

*I*n a kettle of boiling salted water blanch the broccoli for 30 seconds and remove with a slotted spoon. Rinse under cold water and drain. Add the asparagus to the boiling water and blanch for 30 seconds. Remove with slotted spoon, rinse under cold water and drain well.

*C*ombine the dressing ingredients and shake or whisk until well mixed.

*T*oss the beef with some of the dressing and let marinate briefly. Put the pasta, meat and vegetables into an attractive bowl and toss with the remaining dressing. Serve at room temperature or lightly chilled.

Serves 6.

Corned Beef, Crunchy Cabbage and Pasta

This salad will draw raves at your next potluck supper.

8 ounces rotini or other twist pasta

2 cups shredded corned beef

1-1/2 cups coarsely shredded cabbage

1/2 cup shredded carrots

1/2 cup thinly sliced celery

1/4 cup chopped green pepper

1/2 cup chopped green onions

1 recipe Creamy Garlic Sauce
(page 168)

Cook pasta until al dente, drain, rinse with cold water and drain again. Mix with 1/4 cup of the Creamy Garlic Dressing and chill.

Prepare corned beef, cabbage, carrots, celery, green pepper and onions. Add to pasta and toss gently. Add 1/2 cup dressing and mix thoroughly. Chill until serving time and add remaining dressing if necessary.

Serves 6.

Rotelle with Cabbage and Beef

A tasty main-dish salad. Serve it with dark bread and a bright vegetable— such as sliced tomatoes or steamed carrots. You could also substitute left-over ham for the pot roast.

8 ounces rotelle or any twist-type pasta

1/2 pound finely shredded cabbage

2 cups left-over pot roast (or ham), coarsely shredded

2 tablespoons vegetable oil

2 teaspoons caraway seeds

Salt and freshly ground pepper to taste

Dressing

1/4 cup olive oil

2 tablespoons red wine vinegar

1/4 teaspoon salt

1/2 teaspoon sugar

1/2 teaspoon thyme

Cook pasta until al dente, drain well and toss with 1 tablespoon oil.

Heat 1 tablespoon oil in skillet, add beef and fry until edges crisp. Remove from heat and toss with cabbage, caraway seeds and salt and pepper.

Blend dressing ingredients in a small bowl.

Mix cabbage mixture with pasta, add dressing and toss thoroughly. Serve warm or at room temperature.

Serves 6.

Lamb, Green Bean and Orzo Salad

*P*lan ahead: Buy a slightly heavier leg of lamb and enjoy this quick and tasty salad a few days later.

1-1/2 cups orzo or other tiny pasta

2 cups slivers of cooked lamb

1/2 pound green beans, cut into 1 inch pieces

1 small red onion, finely chopped

1 red or green pepper, sliced in thin strips

1/4 cup finely chopped parsley

Salt and freshly ground pepper to taste

Dressing

2/3 cup oil, half olive and half salad oil

3 tablespoons Dijon mustard

2 teaspoons lemon juice

2 cloves garlic, minced

1/2 teaspoon dried rosemary, crushed or 1-1/2 teaspoons fresh

1/2 teaspoon salt

1/2 teaspoon sugar

*C*ook pasta until al dente, drain, rinse under cold water and drain again.

*M*ix dressing ingredients in a large attractive serving bowl and add the pasta, lamb, green beans, onion, sliced pepper and parsley. Mix gently but thoroughly. Chill before serving.

*S*erves 6.

Lamb or Beef with Wheels or Shells

*T*his hearty salad is a "meal in itself," as Mother used to say. Serve with crunchy bread sticks or if you're able, authentic San Francisco sourdough bread. A fruit and cheese platter is a perfect ending.

8 ounces wheels, shells or other small pasta

2 to 3 cups julienned cooked lamb or beef, rare if possible

1 small onion, finely grated

1/2 cup chopped parsley

2 red or green peppers, diced

3 stalks celery, chopped

2 large cucumbers, peeled, seeded and sliced

2 large tomatoes, seeded and coarsely chopped

12 black olives

Mint leaves coarsely chopped for garnish

Dressing

1-1/4 cup salad oil or half salad and half olive

1/4 cup lemon juice

2 tablespoons Dijon mustard

3 cloves garlic, minced

2 tablespoons capers, drained and chopped

2 tablespoons chopped parsley

1/2 teaspoon dried rosemary, crumbled

1/2 teaspoon dried thyme, crushed

1/2 teaspoon salt or to taste

1/2 teaspoon freshly ground pepper

Grated peel of 1/2 lemon

*C*ook pasta until al dente, drain, rinse with cold water and drain again. Transfer to a bowl and toss with 2 tablespoons oil. Chill.

*T*horoughly mix dressing ingredients and marinate the julienned meat in 3/4 cup of the dressing for at least 1 hour.

*P*repare all the vegetables and add to the pasta bowl. At serving time transfer the pasta and vegetables to a shallow serving bowl and toss with the remaining dressing. Surround the outer edge of the bowl with the meat and serve.

*S*erves 6.

Italian Sausage and Vegetables with Wheels

_____

_____

_____

This is a well-rounded nutritious salad that needs only fresh Italian bread to make a complete lunch. A bit of dessert would be nice too.

8 ounces wheels or elbow macaroni

1 pound sweet (mild) Italian sausage

2 tablespoons olive oil

2 medium zucchini, scrubbed and thinly sliced

1 cup chopped green pepper, or a mixture of red and green

1/4 cup chopped pimientos

1/2 cup Italian cured black olives

Dressing

1/2 cup olive oil

2 tablespoons red wine vinegar

1 teaspoon Dijon mustard

2 cloves garlic, minced

1/2 teaspoon salt

1/4 teaspoon freshly ground pepper

1/2 teaspoon crumbled dry basil

*C*ook the pasta until al dente, drain, rinse with cold water and drain again. Transfer to a large bowl and toss with 1 tablespoon olive oil.

*P*ut sausages into a skillet and barely cover with cold water. Bring to a boil, then simmer for 20 minutes. Remove sausage and discard water. Heat 2 tablespoons olive oil in the skillet and lightly brown the sausages. Remove the sausages and let them cool. Slice thinly and add to the pasta.

*T*o the bowl add the prepared zucchini, green and red peppers, the pimientos and the olives. Pour the dressing over the pasta salad and toss well. Serve at room temperature.

*S*erves 6.

Shells, Sausage and Peppers

*P*erfect family main course, quick and easy to fix. When green peppers are out of sight in the markets you might try frozen chopped peppers. Also, add chunks of fresh tomatoes when they are in season; don't bother with the pale winter variety.

8 ounces shell pasta

1-1/2 pounds sweet Italian sausage, or half sweet and half hot

Olive oil, about 1/2 cup

3 green peppers, coarsely chopped

3 cloves garlic, minced

3/4 cup dry white wine or dry vermouth

1/4 cup chopped parsley

Salt and pepper . . . taste before adding pepper

Cook pasta until al dente, drain, rinse with cold water and drain again. In a large bowl toss the pasta with 3 or 4 tablespoons olive oil.

Remove casing from the sausage and break up sausage in a frying pan. Cook until all pink color disappears; drain fat. Add wine and cook down until sausage appears glazed. Set aside.

Saute green peppers, parsley and garlic in 3 tablespoons more olive oil until peppers are just tender but still crisp. Add sausage to mixture and cook briefly.

Toss pepper/sausage mixture with pasta. Add salt and pepper and additional olive oil to taste.

Let flavors blend and serve at room temperature.

Serves 6.

Spaghetti, Italian Sausages and Red Peppers in a Sprightly Sauce

*H*ere is a salad to add pep and punch to any menu. It can also stand alone with the help of chewy, crusty bread and a tossed green salad.

12 ounces spaghetti

1 pound Italian sweet sausage, removed from the casing

4 tablespoons olive oil

3 dried hot chili peppers

1 28-ounce can plum tomatoes, drained and coarsely chopped

3 cloves garlic, minced

2 teaspoons crushed dried oregano

Salt and freshly ground pepper (the amount will be determined by the seasonings in the sausage)

3 large red sweet peppers, thinly sliced (green peppers will do if red are not available)

1/2 cup chopped parsley

1/2 cup coarsely grated Parmesan cheese

*C*ook pasta until al dente, drain and toss with 1 tablespoon olive oil. Transfer to a deep platter.

*H*eat 2 tablespoons olive oil in a skillet and saute the sausage until it loses its pink color. Remove with a slotted spoon and set aside.

*D*iscard all but 1 tablespoon of the pan fat and add to it the remaining 2 tablespoons olive oil. Add the 3 chili peppers and saute until they turn black. Discard peppers, save oil.

*A*dd the tomatoes, oregano, garlic, salt and pepper to the skillet and simmer 15 minutes. Remove from heat and stir in the sliced sweet peppers and the sauteed sausage. Cool to room temperature.

*A*bout 1 hour before serving, add the sauce to the pasta and toss thoroughly. Taste for seasonings.

*A*t serving time sprinkle on the chopped parsley and a few tablespoons of the Parmesan cheese. Pass the remaining cheese separately.

*S*erve at room temperature.

Serves 6.

Primavera with Italian Sausage

This is not quite an authentic primavera because of the addition of the sausage but the contrast of colors makes it an eye-appealing salad.

8 ounces rotelle or other twist pasta

4 sweet Italian sausages

1 hot Italian sausage

1/2 pound fresh asparagus, cut into 2-inch diagonal slices

1/2 pound small mushrooms, left whole or halved

1/2 box cherry tomatoes, halved if too large

1/2 cup chopped parsley

Dressing

2/3 cup olive oil

4 tablespoons red wine vinegar

3 tablespoons lemon juice

3 cloves garlic, minced

1 teaspoon salt

1/2 teaspoon freshly ground black pepper

Remove sausage from casings and saute until it loses its pink color. Remove with a slotted spoon and set aside to cool.

Cook the pasta until al dente, drain and toss with the cooked sausage.

Bring a small amount of water to a boil and add the asparagus. Cook 2 minutes. Drain well and add with the mushrooms and cherry tomatoes to the pasta and sausage mixture. Refrigerate until serving time.

In a small bowl mix the dressing ingredients and set aside.

Just before serving, add the parsley and 1/2 cup dressing to the salad and toss gently. Adjust seasonings and add more dressing as needed.

Serves 6.

Pasta Salad Todi

_____
_____

_____

*S*uzanne's, a Washington, D.C. gourmet carry-out and restaurant, has no idea where the name of this salad came from—only that the salad is a favorite with customers. (Note: Many speciality food stores carry sun-dried tomatoes; these intensely flavored delicacies are well worth seeking out.)

12 ounces rigatoni or other short, tubular pasta

1 red pepper, cut into matchsticks

1 green pepper, cut into matchsticks

1/2 pint cherry tomatoes, halved or quartered depending on size

1/2 cup chopped sun-dried tomatoes

1/3 pound Genoa salami, cut into matchsticks

1/2 pound cervalat or other dry, spicy salami, cut into matchsticks

1/2 cup grated Parmesan cheese

1/4 cup shredded fresh basil, if available

Dressing

1 cup olive oil

1/3 cup balsamic vinegar

2 tablespoons Dijon mustard

1/2 teaspoon oregano

1 or 2 tablespoons oil from the sun-dried tomatoes

Salt and pepper to taste

*C*ook pasta until al dente, drain, rinse with cold water, and drain again.

*T*horoughly blend together the dressing ingredients, either by hand or in a blender or food processor.

*I*n a large bowl, toss together the salad ingredients and the dressing.

*R*efrigerate at least 1 hour. Just before serving, toss again and adjust seasonings if necessary.

*S*erves 6.

Fusilli Salad with Bacon and Cheese

*W*ashington, D.C.'s Food & Co. had a difficult time choosing from among its many pasta salad recipes. We know you'll agree that this one is an excellent selection.

12 ounces fusilli

1 cup freshly grated Parmesan cheese

8 ounces bacon, crisply cooked and crumbled

1/4 cup finely chopped fresh herbs (parsley, chives, basil, tarragon, etc.) or all parsley if other fresh herbs are not available

Dressing

1/2 cup olive oil, or olive and salad mixed

4 tablespoons red wine vinegar

2 teaspoons raspberry vinegar

Salt and freshly ground pepper to taste

*C*ook pasta until al dente, drain, rinse under cold water and drain again.

*T*oss pasta, fresh herbs, Parmesan cheese and most of the dressing. Let sit at room temperature for about 1/2 hour so flavors can blend.

*J*ust before serving, toss again with the bacon and the rest of the dressing. Taste for seasonings.

*S*erves 6.

Pasta Salads with Seafood

Pasta Salads with Seafood

_____
_____
_____

Macaroni and tuna salads were for many of us a staple of childhood. Here, we've taken a good thing several steps farther—pasta salads with seafood that will appeal to the most sophisticated gourmet as well as to children. For the tuna salads, try to find tuna packed in olive oil—and in any event, use solid white meat tuna in oil—for a more luxurious flavor. Find the freshest fish and shellfish you possibly can for the other recipes; it's well worth a special trip to the fish market. Two different methods for steaming mussels and clams are included below.

Steamed Mussels #1

_____
_____
_____

Scrub mussels thoroughly and cut off "beard." Discard any with opened or cracked shells. Cover with cold water and 1 tablespoon salt. Soak for 20 minutes. Preheat oven to 450 degrees. Arrange the drained mussels in one layer on a baking sheet and steam in oven for 7 to 8 minutes until the shells have opened. Discard any unopened mussels.

Steamed Mussels #2

_____
_____
_____

Clean the mussels as in method #1. Place in a heavy kettle or pot with 1/2 cup dry white wine, cover and cook at a high heat for 5 minutes. Leave the cover on for another 5 minutes. Discard any unopened mussels.

Steamed Clams #1

_W_ ash clams thoroughly, cover with cold salted water. Let stand 15 minutes, rinse and repeat two more times. Place in a large kettle, cover, add 2 cups boiling water and bring to a boil. Reduce heat and steam for 10 minutes. Drain; discard any unopened shells.

Steamed Clams #2

_S_ crub the clams thoroughly with a stiff brush under cold running water. Discard any cracked or open shells. Preheat the oven to 450 degrees. Arrange the clams in a single layer on a baking sheet and steam in oven for 7 to 8 minutes or until the shells have opened. Discard any unopened shells.

Pasta and Tuna Suzanne

*T*his colorful yet simple pasta salad, compliments of Suzanne's of Washington, D.C., would make fine luncheon fare, served, perhaps, with crunchy breadsticks and a cool glass of wine.

12 ounces of short pasta, such as shells, macaroni or rigatoni

8-ounce can tuna, preferably packed in olive oil, drained and chunked

1 red pepper, cut into matchsticks

1/2 pound broccoli, broken into bite-sized florets

1/2 cup grated Parmesan cheese

1/4 cup shredded fresh basil

Salt and freshly ground pepper to taste

Dressing

1 cup good quality mayonnaise (homemade would be even better)

2-3 tablespoons tomato sauce (canned is fine)

*C*ook pasta until al dente, drain, rinse under cold water, and drain again.

*D*rop broccoli florets into a large quantity of boiling, salted water and cook for 2 minutes. Drain immediately and rinse under cold water to stop the cooking and set the green; drain well again.

*T*horoughly blend the mayonnaise and tomato sauce.

*I*n a large bowl, toss the salad ingredients, dressing and salt and pepper to taste. Refrigerate at least 1 hour. Just before serving, toss again and adjust seasonings as necessary.

*S*erves 6.

Tuna, Broccoli and Red Peppers with Farfalle

*I*n Italian farfalle means butterfly. This pasta salad is as colorful as the butterflies of Southern Italy and is stunning on a buffet table at any season of the year.

8 ounces farfalle (bow ties)

1 bunch of broccoli

4 red peppers, cut into 1 inch squares, or 2 green peppers and 4 ounces of pimiento, chopped

2 7-1/2 ounce cans solid white tuna in oil, drained and broken into large chunks

1 cup Italian olives or other cured green olives

Dressing

1/2 cup olive oil

3 tablespoons red wine vinegar

2 tablespoons capers, drained

1 teaspoon dried oregano or 1 tablespoon fresh

2 cloves garlic, minced

3/4 teaspoon salt

1/4 teaspoon freshly ground pepper

*C*ook pasta until al dente. Drain, rinse with cold water, drain again and transfer to a large shallow bowl. Toss with 2 tablespoons olive oil.

*C*ut broccoli stems from florets. Peel and slice into 1/2 inch pieces. Divide florets into approximately 1 inch pieces. Cook stems in boiling salted water about 5 minutes. Cook florets in boiling salted water about 3 minutes. Drain both, rinse with cold water and drain again. Gently pat dry with paper towels. Toss florets only with 1/4 cup dressing and chill; reserve. Add the broccoli stems, peppers, olives and tuna to the pasta and toss gently with the remaining dressing. Cover and chill at least 2 hours before serving. Make a border with the broccoli florets before bringing to the table.

*S*erves 6.

Pasta Salad with Tuna and Greek Olives

An easy and refreshing salad for lunch or dinner; accompany with a hot or cold soup and crisp flat bread.

12 ounces rigatoni, penne, or other short pasta

1 7-ounce can tuna in oil, preferably olive, drained

1/2 pound large black Greek olives in brine, drained

1 box cherry tomatoes, cut in half if large

½ cup olive oil, or half olive and half salad

4 tablespoons fresh lemon juice

2 tablespoons drained capers

Salt and pepper to taste

Cook pasta until al dente, drain, rinse under cold water until chilled, drain well and toss with one tablespoon oil.

Pit and chop olives; break tuna into chunks. Put olives, tuna, capers, lemon juice, and olive oil into small bowl. Season with salt and pepper to taste. Mix well.

In large serving bowl, toss pasta, tuna and oil mixture, and tomatoes. Adjust seasonings.

Cover and refrigerate until serving time.

Serves 6.

Tuscany Tuna, Bean and Pasta Salad

To the classic Italian bean and tuna combination we've added pasta.

8 ounces small shell pasta

1 can (16 ounces) small white beans, rinsed and drained

1 can tuna in oil, drained and broken into rough chunks

1 medium red onion, chopped

1 tablespoon chopped parsley

Dressing

1/4 cup olive oil

2 tablespoons fresh lemon juice

1 garlic clove, crushed or finely minced

1/2 teaspoon salt

1/4 teaspoon ground sage

Cook shells to al dente stage, drain well.

Mix all dressing ingredients in large bowl.

Add pasta, tuna, beans, onions, parsley and mix well.

Refrigerate for 4 hours, stirring occasionally.

Serves 6.

Tuna, Pasta and White Bean Salad

Another tuna and bean salad, this one with a creamy dressing and raw spinach leaves.

8 ounces penne or rigatoni

2 7-ounce cans tuna, drained and chunked

1 can (1 pound) small white beans, drained and rinsed

4 cornichons, if available, sliced, or 2 tablespoons good dill pickles, diced

1/4 cup capers, drained

2 long mild fresh peppers, seeded and cut into rings

4 cups spinach leaves, washed, drained, and torn into bite-sized pieces

Dressing

1 cup heavy cream

1/4 cup lemon juice

1/2 teaspoon salt

2 tablespoons chopped chives

Cook pasta until al dente, drain well, and toss with 3 tablespoons vegetable oil.

Combine pasta with tuna, beans, cornichons, capers, peppers and spinach. Chill.

To make dressing, whisk ingredients together and chill. Just before serving, toss salad with the dressing. Adjust seasonings.

Serves 6.

Rotelle and Tuna with Broccoli

This corkscrew-shaped pasta will trap the tasty bits of tuna and vegetables. Serve with bread sticks and a platter of deviled eggs topped with red caviar for a perfect picnic spread.

8 ounces rotelle or shells

1 7-ounce tin tuna fish, drained and flaked

2 cups broccoli florets

1 red sweet pepper, coarsely chopped

1 cup torn watercress leaves and small stems

1 small red onion, thinly sliced

Dressing

2/3 cup olive oil

4 tablespoons herb vinegar

1/2 teaspoon salt

1/2 teaspoon sugar

1/2 teaspoon red pepper flakes

Cook pasta until al dente, drain and toss with 1 tablespoon olive oil. Cool to room temperature.

Cook broccoli in lightly salted water for 3 minutes. Drain well and cool to room temperature.

Mix dressing ingredients.

Add tuna, chopped pepper, cooled broccoli, watercress, onion slices and dressing to pasta and toss gently but thoroughly. Serve at room temperature. If taking on a picnic in summer, chill thoroughly beforehand.

Serves 6.

Tuna and Carrot Pasta Salad

*S*earch out unusual shapes of macaroni-type pasta and use one in this simple salad.

8 ounces short pasta of your choice
1 7-ounce tin tuna, drained and chunked
1 cup thinly sliced carrots
1/2 cup thinly sliced celery
4 green onions, thinly sliced
1/2 cup chopped dill pickles
2 hard-cooked eggs, coarsely chopped
1/2 cup Creamy Garlic Sauce (page 168)
Salt and freshly ground pepper to taste

*C*ook pasta until almost al dente and add sliced carrots for last two minutes of cooking. Drain, rinse with cold water and drain again thoroughly. Toss with 1 tablespoon vegetable oil. Cover and refrigerate at least 1 hour.

*A*dd tuna, celery, pickles, onions, eggs and the Creamy Garlic Sauce. Mix well, taste for salt and pepper and serve.

*S*erves 6.

Pasta Salad with Tuna

A *sophisticated salad that is a far cry from the tuna and noodle salads we ate as children. If you make your own pasta or can buy it fresh, this is the recipe for it.*

12 ounces fettuccine, fresh if possible

6 tablespoons olive oil

2 cloves garlic, finely minced

2 ounces pine nuts

1 cup roughly chopped tomatoes, skinned and seeded (if absolutely necessary, canned plum tomatoes, well drained, may be substituted)

1 can tuna in oil, Italian-style if possible, broken into rough chunks

1/2 red pepper, cut into thin strips (green pepper may be substituted)

6 black olives, pitted and roughly chopped

2 tablespoons chopped parsley

3 tablespoons red wine vinegar

Salt and freshly ground pepper to taste

*H*eat the olive oil in a skillet, add the garlic and pine nuts and saute over low heat about 3 minutes, or until garlic is translucent and pine nuts are golden. Add tomatoes and cook briefly. Turn mixture into a large serving bowl to cool. Do not refrigerate.

*C*ook fettuccine until al dente, drain well. Add pasta to the tomato mixture and toss gently. Add the tuna, pepper strips, black olives, parsley and vinegar. Toss gently and season with salt and plenty of pepper.

*S*erves 6.

Tuna and Garden Delight Farfalle Salad

---

*T*oday's supermarkets carry these garden vegetables all year around now, so you won't have to wait for summer to enjoy this tasty and nutritious salad.

8 ounces farfalle (bowtie) pasta

1 13-ounce can tuna, drained and flaked

1/2 pound broccoli, florets only

1 pound zucchini, quartered and thinly sliced

1/2 pound mushrooms, thinly sliced

2 garlic cloves, minced

2 medium tomatoes, cut in thin wedges or 12 cherry tomatoes, halved

1 medium red onion, thinly sliced

1/3 cup olive oil, divided

1/2 teaspoon oregano, crushed

1 tablespoon chopped fresh basil or 1 teaspoon dried, crushed

1/2 cup mayonnaise

Salt and pepper to taste

*C*ook pasta until al dente and drain thoroughly. Toss with 1 tablespoon olive oil.

*H*eat remaining oil and lightly saute broccoli, zucchini and mushrooms for 2 minutes.

*A*dd minced garlic and herbs, sprinkle with salt and pepper and saute 1 minute longer.

*A*dd vegetables to pasta with tuna, tomatoes, and onions. Mix lightly and add mayonnaise to moisten. Taste for salt and pepper.

*S*erve at room temperature or lightly chilled.

*S*erves 6.

Tart Tuna and Orzo Salad

*A*fter finishing all those Saturday morning chores, reward yourself with this easy and tasty salad for lunch.

1-1/2 cups orzo, ditali or other tiny pasta

1 7-ounce can white tuna packed in water, drained and shredded

1 small red onion, thinly sliced

1 medium to large tomato, seeded and coarsely chopped

1/2 cup chopped parsley

1 teaspoon dried, crushed oregano

3 cups iceberg lettuce in 1/2-inch wide slices

Dressing

1/2 cup olive oil

1/3 cup lemon juice

1/4 cup basil or tarragon vinegar

1/2 to 1 teaspoon salt

1/2 teaspoon freshly ground black pepper

*C*ook pasta until al dente, drain, rinse with cold water and drain again.

*M*ix dressing ingredients in a small bowl.

*A*dd remaining ingredients, except lettuce, to pasta. Pour on half the dressing and toss well. Taste for seasonings and add more dressing as needed.

*M*ake a bed of sliced lettuce on a deep platter, drizzle with some of the dressing and mound the pasta salad in the center. Serve any remaining dressing separately.

*S*erves 6.

Salmon and Pasta with Carrots and Watercress

_____

_____

_____

*B*right colors but subtle flavors and textures. Canned salmon is acceptable though it has a stronger flavor.

8 ounces wheel pasta or small shells

1/2 pound salmon steak simmered 10 minutes in:

1/2 cup dry white wine

1/2 cup water

6 sprigs parsley

1 bay leaf

1 clove garlic

1 teaspoon salt

OR 1 large can of red salmon

3 or 4 carrots

1 cup boiling salted water

1/2 bunch watercress, coarse stems removed

1 cup Italian olives, pitted and halved

2 tablespoons capers, rinsed

Dressing

1/2 cup olive oil or half olive and half salad

1/4 cup lemon juice

1 tablespoon Dijon-style mustard

1 clove garlic, minced

1 teaspoon crushed dried tarragon

1/2 teaspoon salt

1/4 teaspoon freshly ground black pepper

*C*ook the pasta to al dente stage, drain, run under cold water and drain again.

*C*ook fresh salmon as directed. Remove skin and bones, coarsely flake, and refrigerate. Or drain and remove any skin and bones from canned salmon, coarsely flake and refrigerate.

*C*ook carrots in boiling salted water for 10 minutes, drain and slice into 1/4 inch rounds.

*I*n a large attractive bowl mix the dressing ingredients and add the cooked pasta, chilled salmon, carrots, watercress and olives. Toss gently and chill lightly before serving.

*S*erves 6.

Summer Salmon and Shells

A salad to remind you of summer. A nice luncheon dish served with a hot green vegetable, French bread, and a crisp white wine.

8 ounces small shell pasta

2 cups shredded iceberg lettuce

1/2 cup pitted ripe olive halves

1 box cherry tomatoes, halved

2 cucumbers, peeled, halved and seeded, then sliced into half rounds

1 large can salmon, drained and chunked (remove bones and skin)

Dressing

1-1/2 cups mayonnaise

1/4 cup milk

1 tablespoon chopped onion

1/2 teaspoon dillweed

1 tablespoon vinegar

1 teaspoon salt

Mix dressing ingredients together thoroughly. Chill.

Cook pasta shells, drain well and toss with 1 tablespoon oil and the black olive halves.

In large glass bowl, layer lettuce, shells and olive mixture, tomatoes, cucumbers, and salmon. Pour 3/4 cup dressing over top.

Chill. Toss at table and pass remaining dressing.

Serves 6.

Any Season Salmon and Shell Salad

---

*Y*ou probably have the makings for this salad in your cupboard or refrigerator right now. If not, substitutions are easy.

8 ounces shell pasta (or other macaroni type)

1 large can red or pink salmon, well drained and flaked

1 cup thinly sliced carrots

1/2 cup chopped celery

1/2 cup pimiento stuffed olives, halved

1/2 package frozen peas, blanched with boiling water and well drained

1/2 cup chopped parsley

1 small onion, chopped or 4 green onions, chopped

1/2 red or green pepper, julienned

Dressing

1/2 cup salad oil, or half salad and half olive

4 tablespoons lemon juice

1 tablespoon vinegar

2 teaspoons Dijon mustard

1 tablespoon dillweed or to taste

1/2 teaspoon salt, or more to taste

1/4 teaspoon freshly ground pepper

*C*ook pasta until al dente, drain well, mix with 1 tablespoon oil and refrigerate.

*W*hisk all dressing ingredients in a small bowl or shake well in a covered jar.

*A*dd salmon, vegetables and almost all the dressing to the chilled pasta. Chill another 1/2 hour before serving.

*T*aste for seasoning and add more dressing if needed to moisten.

*S*erves 6.

Fish and Thin Noodles, Oriental Style

*A*n economical but impressive dish to wow your dinner guests. Chinese noodles, sesame oil, and fresh bean sprouts can be found in Oriental food stores and in large supermarkets.

8 ounces spaghettini or thin Chinese egg noodles

1-1/2 pounds firm fish fillets: tilefish, cod, haddock, etc.

1/4 cup lemon juice

1 tablespoon salad oil

2 tablespoons sesame oil

2 cups fresh bean sprouts

1 large carrot, grated

1/4 cup chopped green onion tops

Dressing

6 tablespoons chicken broth

6 tablespoons soy sauce

2 tablespoons smooth peanut butter

3 teaspoons sesame oil

1 tablespoon white vinegar

2 teaspoons sugar

2 teaspoons minced garlic

2 teaspoons grated fresh ginger

1/2 teaspoon Tabasco sauce, or to taste

*P*ut the fillets, lemon juice and water to cover in a stainless steel or Teflon-coated pan and poach, at barely a simmer, for 5 to 7 minutes.

*C*ool the fish in the liquid, then drain, skin if necessary and flake.

*C*ook pasta until al dente, drain well. Transfer to a large shallow dish or platter and toss with 1 tablespoon salad oil and 2 teaspoons sesame oil.

*B*lanch the bean sprouts in boiling water for 30 seconds. Drain and rinse under cold water and drain again.

*I*n a small bowl thoroughly mix the dressing ingredients.

*A*rrange the bean sprouts and shredded carrots over the noodles, top with the flaked fish.

*P*our the dressing on top and garnish with the chopped green onion tops. Serve lightly chilled.

*S*erves 6.

Seaside Spaghetti

On a warm summer day this melange of flavors will remind you of the sunny Mediterranean. Serve with crisp Italian bread to sop up the flavorful juices.

12 ounces spaghettini·or linguine

1/2 pound fillet of sole or flounder

1/2 pound small raw shrimp

6 fresh tomatoes, peeled, seeded and coarsely chopped or 1 16-ounce can Italian plum tomatoes, drained and coarsely chopped

1/2 cup olive oil

1 medium onion, finely chopped

1/4 cup dry white wine

3 teaspoons fresh basil, chopped or 1-1/2 teaspoon dried basil, crushed

3 cloves garlic, minced

2 teaspoons fresh marjoram or 1 teaspoon dried marjoram, crushed

Salt and pepper to taste

1/2 cup chopped fresh parsley

*C*ook pasta until al dente. Drain, rinse under cold water and drain again. Toss with 1 tablespoon olive oil to prevent sticking. Chill.

*P*oach fish fillet in lightly salted water with bay leaf, about 5 minutes; cool and flake.

*C*ook shrimp in boiling salted water with small onion for 3 minutes, drain, shell and cool.

*S*aute onion in hot olive oil until barely tender, add garlic and cook briefly. Add wine and herbs and cook about 1 minute, just to boil off alcohol. Add tomatoes and cook 5 minutes over medium heat. Add salt and pepper to taste. (Remember that cold sauce needs heavier seasoning.)

*R*efrigerate until cold, then add fish and shrimp.

*A*rrange pasta on a deep platter, spoon seafood sauce on top and sprinkle with chopped fresh parsley.

*S*erves 6.

Seafood, Pasta and Vegetable Salad

If shrimp is too expensive, simply double the amount of fish. To make up for the color the shrimp would have provided, add a small jar of drained, sliced pimiento.

8 ounces mostaccioli

1 pound flounder fillets

1 pound shrimp

1/2 cup dry white wine

1/4 cup chopped scallion

1/2 teaspoon salt

2 medium zucchini, julienned

2 leeks, white part only, sliced thinly

1-1/2 cups shelled raw peas, or 1 box frozen peas, thawed only

Dressing

1 cup peeled, shredded cucumber

1/2 teaspoon salt

1 cup sour cream

2 teaspoons dillweed

Dash of cardomom (optional)

*C*ook pasta to al dente stage, drain well and toss with 2 tablespoons vegetable oil to prevent sticking. Chill.

*S*immer, covered, the flounder and shrimp in the wine, scallions, and salt for 5 minutes or less. Cool in liquid, then drain well.

*C*ut fish into bite-sized pieces; shell and devein shrimp. Chill.

*T*o make dressing, mix the cucumber and the salt and let stand in colander for one hour. Squeeze dry and mix with the sour cream, dillweed and the optional cardomom.

*T*oss pasta, seafood and vegetables with the dressing. Adjust seasonings.

*S*erves 6.

Delicate Oriental Noodle and Seafood Salad

___

A light but vibrant salad perfect for a first course or a hot weather main course. Double the amount of shrimp and scallops to serve 6 as a main course.

8 ounces cellophane noodles or vermicelli

1/2 pound small raw shrimp

1/2 pound scallops

1 cup thinly sliced celery

1 handful watercress leaves and stems

1 whole pimiento, sliced

1 large cucumber, halved lengthwise, seeded and sliced thinly crosswise

Dressing

1/2 cup lemon juice

1/2 cup chopped green onion, tops and bottoms

2 tablespoons sesame oil

1 tablespoon soy sauce

1/2 teaspoon salt

1/2 teaspoon hot chili oil, or Tabasco sauce

1/2 teaspoon sugar

Cook cellophane noodles or vermicelli according to package directions. Drain well, run under cold water and drain thoroughly. Add half of dressing and toss lightly.

Simmer shrimp and scallops in boiling water just to cover, about 2 minutes. Drain, shell and devein shrimp. Slice scallops into 1/2 inch rounds. If using bay scallops, leave them whole or cut in half. Add to the noodles with the celery, pimiento, watercress, and the remaining dressing. Toss and chill until serving time. Divide among six (preferably glass) salad plates and garnish with the cucumber slices.

Six first-course servings.

Rice Noodles and Shrimp with Vegetables

Start with an assortment of appetizers from your local Chinese restaurant. This Oriental-style pasta salad followed by a variety of sherbets with fortune cookies make for an easy Sunday night supper.

8 ounces rice noodles or bean thread noodles

12 ounces shrimp, cooked and peeled

10-ounce package fresh spinach, torn into pieces

1/4 pound fresh mushrooms, sliced

4 green onions, sliced diagonally into 1/2 inch pieces

1 medium zucchini, julienned into 1-inch lengths

8-10 radishes, sliced

Dressing

1/4 cup salad oil

1 clove garlic, crushed

2 tablespoons soy sauce

2 tablespoons white wine vinegar

1/4 teaspoon Chinese five-spice powder

2 teaspoons sesame seeds, for garnish

Cook noodles briefly, drain, rinse with cold water and drain thoroughly. Toss with 1 tablespoon salad oil.

Shake dressing ingredients in a covered jar. Cut shrimp into 1-inch pieces. Add shrimp and vegetables to the noodles. Add the dressing and toss well.

Sprinkle with sesame seeds. Serve lightly chilled.

Serves 6.

Herb-Dressed Shrimp and Pasta Salad

Influenced by Northern Italian cuisine, this salad is enhanced by a delicate but distinctive herb dressing. It is light enough for a first course, but would do nicely as the entree on a warm summer evening.

12 ounces small twist pasta or small shells

1 pound cold cooked shrimp, shelled and deveined

1/2 cup chopped parsley

Dressing

1/2 cup olive oil, divided

4 tablespoons lemon juice

1 teaspoon crushed tarragon

1/4 teaspoon crushed rosemary

1/2 teaspoon salt, or more to taste

1/8 teaspoon Tabasco sauce, or more to taste

Cook pasta until al dente, drain well and toss with 2 tablespoons oil. Set aside to cool.

Chop the shrimp into small pieces.

Thoroughly mix the remaining oil, lemon juice, herbs, salt and Tabasco sauce. Taste and adjust seasonings.

In a serving bowl, toss the pasta, shrimp, dressing and parsley. Cover and let flavors blend about 1/2 hour. (Refrigerate if salad won't be served for more than 1/2 hour.) Just before serving, toss again.

Serves 6.

Shrimp, Ham and Penne with Dilled Vinaigrette

_____

_____

_____

A *lettuce-lined shallow bowl of this salad, a platter of cold fried chicken, crunchy bread and your favorite beverage and dessert make perfect picnic fare.*

8 ounces penne or rotini

1/2 pound cooked, diced shrimp

1/2 pound ham steak, cooked and julienned

2 hard-cooked eggs, chopped

1 small red onion, thinly sliced

1 cucumber, peeled, seeded and sliced

1/2 cup sliced ripe olives

2 ounce jar sliced pimiento, drained

1 recipe Dill Vinaigrette (page 162)

Cook pasta until al dente, drain, rinse with cold water and drain again. Toss with 1 tablespoon olive oil and refrigerate while preparing remaining ingredients.

Add shrimp, ham, eggs, onion, cucumber, olives, pimiento and the Dill Vinaigrette to the pasta. Toss well and serve lightly chilled.

Serves 6.

Low-Calorie Linguine with Shrimp-Yogurt Sauce

A light and tasty first course or luncheon dish. Instead of a calorie-laden cream sauce, this recipe calls for yogurt. The shrimp also keep the calories down while adding a touch of luxury.

12 ounces linguine
1 pound shrimp, cooked and peeled
1/2 cup chopped parsley
1/2 cup sliced scallions, including green
2 cups plain yogurt
Salt and pepper to taste
1 teaspoon lemon zest, finely grated
1 teaspoon crushed tarragon
1/4 teaspoon thyme
1/4 teaspoon paprika

Cook pasta to al dente stage, drain well and toss with 1 tablespoon salad oil.

In a blender container, combine half the cooked shrimp and the remaining ingredients. Blend until almost smooth. Adjust seasonings.

Toss pasta, reserved shrimp and dressing thoroughly. Let sit at room temperature about 1/2 hour to allow flavors to blend before serving.

Serves 6.

Orzo and Shrimp Salad

Serve this light salad in lettuce cups as a first course or to your card group for lunch or an evening snack.

1-1/2 cups orzo or other tiny pasta

3/4 pound fresh medium shrimp (frozen will do if necessary)

2 cups simmering water seasoned with 1 teaspoon salt, 4 peppercorns, 1 stalk celery with leaves, 2 whole cloves

4 stalks celery with leaves, finely chopped

1/4 cup minced parsley

1 tablespoon capers, rinsed and drained for garnish

Dressing

1/3 cup mayonnaise

1/3 cup olive oil

3 tablespoons white wine vinegar

1/2 teaspoon salt

1/4 teaspoon freshly ground pepper

1/2 teaspoon dillweed

Cook pasta until al dente, drain, toss with 1 tablespoon olive oil and chill.

Simmer the unpeeled or frozen shrimp in the seasoned water just until pink or defrosted and cooked through. Drain, shell and cut into coarse pieces. Chill.

Mix dressing ingredients and toss in serving bowl with pasta, shrimp, parsley and celery. Taste for seasonings. Before serving garnish with capers.

Serves 6.

Pasta- and Shrimp-Stuffed Tomato Shells

A *bright red tomato shell nestled in a tender bibb lettuce leaf makes an attractive first course; with the addition of creamed avocado soup and crisp French bread, it's a satisfying luncheon entree.*

1 cup orzo pasta or other tiny pasta

6 ripe tomatoes

3/4 pound shrimp, cooked, shelled and coarsely chopped

1 large cucumber, peeled, seeded and coarsely chopped

1/4 cup finely chopped green pepper

1/4 cup finely chopped green onions

1/2 teaspoon salt

1/2 cup Dill Vinaigrette (page 162)

*H*ollow out tomatoes and drain well upside down. (Reserve tomato pulp for another use.)

*C*ook pasta until al dente, drain, rinse with cold water and drain again. Mix with 1 tablespoon of the Dill Vinaigrette dressing.

*A*dd the shrimp, remaining dressing, vegetables and salt to the pasta and refrigerate until well chilled.

*F*ill tomato shells and arrange on lettuce-lined salad plates.

Serves 6.

Jumbo Shells Stuffed with Crabmeat

This is quite an elegant first course. Serve with lemon wedges and thinly sliced toasted French bread.

12 jumbo pasta shells (cook a few extra as a couple usually break)

1 pound crabmeat (lump or backfin, preferably)

2/3 cup olive oil, divided

1/4 cup lemon juice, divided

1 tablespoon drained and rinsed capers, chopped

2 tablespoons pine nuts or slivered almonds, coarsely chopped

2 tablespoons minced parsley

1/2 teaspoon salt, or more to taste

1/8 teaspoon cayenne pepper

1/2 cup Basic Vinaigrette
(page 160)

Boston or bibb lettuce leaves

Watercress sprigs for garnish

Cook pasta shells, gently, until al dente. Remove with a slotted spoon to drain. While still hot mix carefully with 1 tablespoon olive oil, 2 tablespoons lemon juice and 1 tablespoon parsley.

Drain any juice from crabmeat, discard juice. Mix the crab with remaining olive oil, lemon juice, capers, nuts, parsley, salt and cayenne pepper. Stuff shells and refrigerate until shortly before serving.

Arrange lettuce on salad plates, add two shells per plate and drizzle lightly with vinaigrette dressing. Garnish with watercress sprigs and lemon wedges.

Serves 6.

Herbed Scallops and Linguine

*E*legant first course, garnished with sprigs of fresh dill and accompanied by short sesame bread sticks for texture contrast.

1/2 pound linguine

1-1/2 pounds bay scallops (1-1/2 pints) or sea scallops, quartered after cooking

Dressing

1-1/2 cups good mayonnaise, homemade not essential

2 teaspoons capers, washed in cold water, drained and minced

1-1/2 tablespoons fresh herbs (dill, thyme or tarragon)

2 tablespoons minced parsley

1/2 teaspoon salt

1/4 teaspoon freshly ground pepper

Minced chives or finely chopped green onion tops to sprinkle on top of salad

*C*ook pasta until al dente. Drain, rinse with cold water and drain again. Toss with 1 tablespoon oil and chill.

*W*ash and drain scallops. Place them in a large frying pan and barely cover with cold water. Bring to a boil, lower heat and simmer 1 minute. Drain and refrigerate while preparing the dressing.

*S*tir the dressing ingredients together and combine with the scallops. Refrigerate if not using immediately.

*A*t serving time mix the scallops gently with the linguine and divide among six salad plates. Sprinkle with chives and garnish with dill or other herb sprigs. Serve chilled.

*S*erves 6.

Fettuccine with Scallops and Langostinos

*S*callops marinated in lime juice, langostinos and a piquant dressing of lime and fresh coriander make this salad a refreshing first course for summer dinner parties. A specialty of Fete Accomplie Catering, Washington, D.C.

12 ounces fettuccine, homemade if possible

1/2 pound bay scallops

1 12-ounce package frozen langostinos, or good flavored cooked jumbo shrimp

1 cup fresh lime juice

1/2 cup olive oil

2 tablespoons chopped fresh coriander

Salt and freshly ground pepper to taste

Pinch of sugar

*M*arinate scallops in 2/3 cup fresh lime juice 3 to 4 hours or overnight in the refrigerator.

*D*efrost langostinos or cook shrimp.

*C*ook pasta until al dente, drain, rinse with cold water and drain again. Pat pasta dry with paper towels.

*D*rain scallops and discard marinade.

*M*ix 1/3 cup lime juice, oil, salt, pepper and sugar in a small bowl. Add finely chopped coriander. Taste for seasoning.

*A*dd all ingredients to pasta and toss lightly. Serve at room temperature or lightly chilled.

*S*erves 6.

Scallop, Green Bean and Wagonwheel Salad

*F*resh dill is a must for optimum enjoyment of this refreshing seafood salad.

8 ounces wagonwheels or shells

1-1/2 pounds large sea scallops

1 cup dry white wine

1 small white onion, sliced

2 lemon slices

1 bay leaf

1/2 pound green beans, blanched 2 minutes and chilled

4 scallions, sliced into rounds, including some of the green

Red lettuce (raddichio), if available, or green lettuce leaves

Dressing

3/4 cup olive oil

1/4 cup white wine vinegar

1 teaspoon salt

White pepper to taste

1 teaspoon sugar

1/4 cup dill sprigs

1 teaspoon dillseed

*M*ake the dressing first; it should stand at room temperature several hours to let the flavor develop. Shake dressing ingredients together in covered jar until thick. Let stand, then shake again.

*C*ook wagonwheels until al dente, drain well, and toss with 2 tablespoons olive oil.

*S*immer the sea scallops in the wine, onion slices, lemon slices and bay leaf for 10 minutes. Cool in the liquid, drain. Slice scallops thinly. Toss with the pasta and the vegetables.

*A*dd the dressing, by the spoonful, tossing well after each addition until salad is well coated. Adjust seasonings. Serve chilled or at room temperature on the lettuce leaves.

*S*ix appetizer servings.

Curried Mussel Salad with Tiny Pasta

Use the smallest size pasta you can find, such as ave maria, ditalini rigati, or orzo. However, in a pinch, the smallest shells will do.

1-1/2 cups tiny pasta

4 quarts steamed mussels

1 10-ounce package frozen tiny peas, thawed

1/2 cup chopped celery leaves or parsley

Curried French Dressing

1/2 cup olive oil

2 tablespoons wine vinegar

2 teaspoons minced green onions

1 teaspoon curry powder

1/2 teaspoon salt, or more to taste

Curried Mayonnaise Dressing

1/3 cup mayonnaise

2 teaspoons curry powder

1/2 teaspoon salt

Cook the pasta until al dente. Drain, rinse with cold water and drain again. Toss with 2 tablespoons of the Curried French Dressing.

Clean and cook the mussels according to the directions on page 117; cool and discard shells and any black rims. In a salad bowl toss with 1/4 cup of the Curried French Dressing.

Pour boiling water over the peas and drain.

In the salad bowl combine the pasta with the peas and mussels and remaining French dressing.

Mix the Curried Mayonnaise Dressing ingredients and carefully fold into the salad ingredients. Chill at least 2 hours and sprinkle with the chopped celery leaves or chopped parsley before serving.

Serves 6.

Mussels Marinara with Linguine

A *tantalizing blend of rich Italian seasonings combined with inexpensive mussels and pasta. A basket of Italian bread, to dip in the flavorful sauce, and a crisp green salad will make a satisfying meal for family or friends.*

12 ounces linguine

4 quarts mussels

1 large onion, thinly sliced

3 cloves garlic, finely minced

1/4 cup olive oil

1 lemon, thinly sliced

1 28-ounce can Italian plum tomatoes

1/2 of a 6-ounce can of tomato paste

10 leaves fresh basil, chopped or
1 tablespoon dried basil

1 teaspoon dried oregano

1/8 teaspoon cayenne pepper

1/2 teaspoon freshly ground black pepper

2 teaspoons salt

1 cup dry red wine

Chopped flat leaf (Italian) parsley for garnish, or regular if Italian is not available

*C*lean the mussels according to the directions given on page 117.

*S*aute the onion and garlic in the olive oil in a large pot. Add the lemon slices when the onion is soft. Whirl the tomatoes and tomato paste in a food processor or mash lightly to break up. Add to the pot with the basil, oregano, red and black pepper and salt. Simmer over low heat, stirring occasionally, about 25 minutes. Add the wine and simmer 15 to 20 minutes more.

*C*ook the linguine until al dente and drain well. Turn out into a shallow bowl.

*W*hile pasta is cooking, add the mussels to the simmering sauce and cook about 6 to 8 minutes, until the shells open. Discard any unopened shells. Pour the sauce over the pasta and mix very gently. Allow to stand at room temperature about 1/2 hour before serving. Sprinkle with the chopped parsley.

*S*erves 6.

Fettuccine and Mussel Salad

T his sophisticated and attractive salad could be preceded by chilled consomme with julienned vegetables and accompanied by the best French bread available.

12 ounces green fettuccine—fresh if available

4 pounds (about 4 quarts) mussels

1/4 cup minced onion

1/4 cup minced celery

1/4 cup chopped green onions

3 cloves minced garlic

2 teaspoons minced fresh thyme or 1/2 teaspoon dried

1/4 cup unsalted butter

1/3 cup dry white wine

1-1/2 cups heavy cream

1/2 cup chopped parsley

Salt and pepper to taste

2 tablespoons olive oil

Clean the mussels according to directions on page 117.

In a stainless steel pot saute the celery, onion, green onion, garlic and thyme until the vegetables are soft. Add the mussels and dry white wine. Bring to a boil, cover and steam about 6 minutes or until the shells have opened. Discard any unopened mussels. Transfer the mussels to a large bowl. Reserve 12 mussels in their shells and shell remainder. Strain the broth into a pot and reduce it over high heat to about 1/2 cup. Stir in the heavy cream and simmer until slightly thickened. Remove from the heat and stir in the chopped parsley; taste for salt and pepper. Stir in the reserved shelled and unshelled mussels and let the sauce cool. Refrigerate.

Cook the fettuccine until al dente, drain, rinse under cold water and drain again. Transfer to a large serving bowl and toss with the olive oil. Cool to room temperature.

Pour the mussel sauce over the fettuccine and toss well before serving.

Serves 6.

Mussels and Pasta in Sauce Verte

A first course of distinction, this dish uses two of the basic sauces found in the chapter on dressings.

8 ounces medium shells
18-24 fresh, tightly closed mussels
1/2 cup water
1 clove garlic, crushed
1/2 cup Basic Vinaigrette (page 160)
1 recipe Sauce Verte (page 166)

Cook pasta to al dente stage, drain well and toss with the Basic Vinaigrette. Refrigerate at least one hour.

Clean the mussels according to directions on page 117. Place mussels in large skillet, add water and garlic. Cook, covered, over high heat 5 to 8 minutes. Shake skillet frequently so mussels will cook uniformly. When mussels open, remove with slotted spoon to large bowl. Cover and refrigerate 1 hour.

Make one recipe Sauce Verte. Put 1 teaspoon sauce on each chilled mussel in shell. Reserve remaining sauce.

Turn chilled pasta onto serving platter and mound filled mussels in the middle. Pass reserved sauce.

Six appetizer servings.

Shell Pasta with Mussels and Broccoli

*H*ere is an inexpensive but sophisticated salad that will be a crowd-pleaser on summer buffet tables.

8 ounces shell pasta

4 quarts mussels

1/2 pound broccoli

1/4 pound mushrooms, thinly sliced

2 cloves garlic, minced

4 green onions, chopped

1 teaspoon tarragon

1 teaspoon thyme

1 cup dry white wine

2 teaspoons salt

2 tablespoons chopped parsley, for garnish

Dressing

1/2 cup liquid from mussels, reduced and strained

1/2 cup olive oil

1 teaspoon Dijon-style mustard

1/2 teaspoon freshly ground pepper

Salt to taste

*C*lean the mussels according to the directions on page 117. Transfer the mussels to a stainless steel pot and add the garlic, onions, herbs, salt and wine. Bring to a boil, cover and steam about 6 minutes or until the shells have opened. Remove the mussels and discard any unopened shells. Strain the liquid and reduce to 1/2 cup. Reserve for the dressing.

*C*ook the pasta until al dente, drain, rinse with cold water and drain again. Toss with 1 tablespoon olive oil.

*C*ut away heavy stems on broccoli and peel the remaining stems. Slice the stems into 1/4-inch pieces and break the heads into small florets.

*R*emove the cooled mussels from the shells and add to the pasta with the broccoli, mushrooms and 3/4 cup of the dressing. Mix well and refrigerate.

*B*efore serving taste to see if additional dressing is needed. Add the chopped parsley and toss gently.

*S*erves 6.

Shells with Shrimp, Scallops and Snow Peas

This light and tangy salad will whet any appetite when served as a first course. Or it can stand alone as a refreshing luncheon dish.

8 ounces shell pasta

1 pound small or medium shrimp

1 pound scallops

1/4 pound snow peas or 1 10-ounce box frozen snow peas

2 cucumbers, peeled, seeded and sliced

4 celery stalks, thinly sliced

1 small onion

4 peppercorns

2 teaspoons salt

Dressing

1/2 cup white wine vinegar

1/4 cup olive oil

1/4 cup water

1/4 cup soy sauce

3 tablespoons dry mustard

3 tablespoons sesame oil

3 tablespoons dry sherry

1-1/2 tablespoons sugar

Salt to taste

Cook shrimp in boiling water with onion, peppercorns and salt until just pink, about 3 minutes. Drain, cool and peel.

Cook scallops in simmering water, lightly salted, just until translucent. If using large scallops, quarter; add to shrimp and set aside to cool.

Put fresh or thawed snow peas in a colander and pour boiling water over them. Transfer to a small bowl, add the cucumbers and toss lightly.

Cook pasta until al dente; drain; rinse under cold water; drain again.

While pasta is cooking, combine dressing ingredients. Lightly mix the shrimp and scallops with the snow peas, cucumbers and celery and half of the dressing.

Toss the drained pasta with the remaining dressing and arrange in a shallow bowl or on salad plates. Mound the seafood and vegetable mixture in the center of the pasta bed.

Serves 6.

Linguine and Mixed Seafood Salad

A special trip to the fishmonger—or preferably the wharf—is well worth
it for this stunning summertime treat.

8 ounces linguine

1-1/2 pounds small squid

4 pounds mussels

2 pounds littleneck clams or other small
hard-shelled clams

Olive oil

Dressing

1/4 cup lemon juice

1/2 cup olive oil

2 cloves garlic, minced

1/2 teaspoon salt or more to taste

1/4 teaspoon freshly ground pepper

Garnish

1 red onion, thinly sliced

1/3 cup Italian or regular parsley, chopped

Lemon juice and salt and pepper to taste

*C*ook the linguine until al dente. Drain, rinse with cold water and drain
again. Toss with 2 tablespoons olive oil. Clean and cook the mussels and
clams according to the directions on page 117. Do not shell.

*H*ave fish market clean and skin the squid. Wash the squid thoroughly;
cut the bodies into 1/4 inch rings and chop the tentacles finely. In a large
skillet saute the squid for 2 minutes in enough oil to cover the bottom of
the pan. Transfer to a large glass salad bowl.

*T*o the bowl add the pasta, the steamed, unshelled mussels and the
steamed, unshelled clams.

*T*oss with the salad dressing and chill at least 3 hours. Before serving
taste for lemon juice and salt and pepper. Add onion rings and parsley
and toss again.

*S*erves 6.

Fusilli and Mussels in Spinach Sauce

*H*ere is an elegant—or earthy—accompaniment to your next seafood dinner or buffet table. All the preparations are done early in the day and it's just toss-and-serve at the last minute.

12 ounces fusilli

4 pounds fresh mussels

1 cup dry white wine

1/4 cup lemon juice

1/2 cup chopped parsley

1 teaspoon grated fresh ginger or 2 teaspoons powdered ginger

1 teaspoon salt

Spinach Sauce

1-1/2 cups tightly packed fresh spinach, coarse stems removed

1/2 cup parsley, coarse stems removed

6 green onions, cut into 1 inch pieces

1 cup good quality mayonnaise

1/4 cup lemon juice

1/2 teaspoon fresh ginger or 1/2 teaspoon powdered ginger or more to taste

1 teaspoon salt

1/2 teaspoon freshly ground black pepper

Clean and cook the mussels with the wine, lemon juice, parsley, ginger and salt according to directions on page 117.

Cool and remove mussels from their shells. Refrigerate until serving time with some of the strained cooking liquor.

Cook pasta until al dente, drain, rinse with cold water and drain again; toss with 1 tablespoon olive oil. Cover tightly and refrigerate.

In a food processor or blender puree the spinach, parsley and green onions. Add the remaining ingredients and blend thoroughly. Refrigerate.

At serving time toss the pasta with about 1/2 cup of the sauce. Drain mussels and mix with about 1/2 cup of the sauce. Top the pasta with the mussels and pass the remaining Spinach Sauce.

Serves 6.

Shells and Swedish Herring Salad

*H*ere is an updated version of the Swedish favorite, Sillsallad. Serve with
a hearty black bread and a crock of unsalted butter.

8 ounces shell pasta

2 cups pickled herring, cut into small
pieces

1 cup diced boiled potatoes

2 cups diced cooked beets

2 medium apples, peeled and diced

1/2 cup chopped onions

1 teaspoon dried dillweed or 2 tablespoons
chopped fresh dill leaves

1 medium cucumber, not peeled, thinly
sliced for garnish

Dressing

2 cups good quality mayonnaise

1 teaspoon salt

1-1/2 tablespoons sugar

1/2 teaspoon freshly ground black pepper

*C*ook pasta until al dente, drain, rinse with cold water and drain again.

*A*dd herring, potatoes, beets, apples, onions and dill to pasta. Mix lightly.

*M*ix dressing ingredients in a small bowl and pour over pasta and herring
mixture. Mix well and refrigerate until serving time.

*A*rrange salad on a bed of lettuce leaves on a platter.

*S*erves 6.

Chilled Squid Salad with Spaghettini

A n elegant first course. Serve on clear glass salad plates and garnish with lemon rounds and parsley sprigs.

12 ounces spaghettini

1 pound cleaned squid, fresh or thawed frozen

3/4 cup olive oil, divided

1/4 cup fresh lemon juice

2 cloves garlic, minced

1/4 cup parsley, minced

1 tablespoon chopped fresh basil or 1 teaspoon dried

Salt and pepper to taste

Cook spaghettini until al dente, drain and toss with 1/4 cup olive oil. Refrigerate until 1 hour before serving.

Slice the cleaned squid bodies into 1/4-inch rings; slice fins and tentacles into thin strips. Bring a pot of water to a boil, add squid and boil gently, uncovered, for about 15 minutes or until squid is tender. Drain well. In a medium bowl, mix together the squid, garlic, parsley, basil, lemon juice and 1/2 cup olive oil. Cover and refrigerate at least overnight. About 1 hour before serving, toss the spaghettini and the squid mixture together, and salt and pepper to taste; refrigerate. Just before serving, taste for seasonings and adjust if necessary.

Serves 6.

Salad Dressings and Sauces

Salad Dressings and Sauces

_W_e've included a number of dressings and sauces—in addition to those with each recipe—so you can invent your own pasta salads. Many of these dressings would also be good on a simple green salad or even cold rice or vegetables.

Basic Vinaigrette

3/4 cup olive oil or half olive and half salad

1/4 cup vinegar

1 teaspoon dry mustard or 2 teaspoons
Dijon mustard

1 teaspoon salt

1/2 teaspoon freshly ground black pepper

*W*hisk ingredients together in a small bowl.

*T*he amount of salt may seem excessive but remember that chilling lessens the effectiveness of seasonings and herbs.

*M*akes about 1 cup.

Herbed Vinaigrette

2 tablespoons white wine vinegar

1/3 cup good olive oil

1/2 teaspoon Dijon-style mustard

1 tablespoon finely chopped parsley

2 teaspoons fresh, finely chopped tarragon
or 1 teaspoon crumbled dry tarragon

2 teaspoons minced chives

2 teaspoons minced chervil, if available
or 1 teaspoon dried basil

1/2 teaspoon salt

Fresh ground pepper to taste, about
1/4 teaspoon

*I*n a small bowl whisk the vinegar, mustard and salt and pepper together. Add the olive oil and beat again. Stir in the fresh or dried herbs. Taste for seasoning.

*M*akes about 3/4 cup.

Dill Vinaigrette

1/2 cup olive oil or half olive and half salad oil

3 tablespoons white wine vinegar

1 tablespoon Dijon-style mustard

1/2 teaspoon salt

Freshly ground black pepper, about 1/4 teaspoon

1/4 teaspoon sugar

3 tablespoons snipped fresh dill

*I*n a small bowl whisk together the vinegar, mustard, salt, pepper and sugar. Add the oil and the dill and whisk until well incorporated.

*M*akes about 3/4 cup.

Sesame Seed Vinaigrette

2 cloves garlic, minced

2 teaspoons sesame seeds

1/2 cup olive oil

3 tablespoons wine vinegar

1/2 teaspoon salt

Freshly ground pepper to taste, about
1/4 teaspoon

*I*n a small skillet saute the garlic and sesame seeds in the olive oil until the seeds are lightly browned. Strain the olive oil into a small bowl and put the garlic and sesame seeds into another small bowl. Add the vinegar, salt and pepper to the garlic and seeds and whisk together. Add the oil and whisk again; taste for seasoning.

*M*akes about 1/2 cup.

Tarragon and Soy Vinaigrette

1/2 cup olive oil

1/4 cup tarragon vinegar

1/4 cup soy sauce

1 tablespoon snipped fresh tarragon or
1 teaspoon dried tarragon, crushed

1/2 teaspoon dry mustard

1/4 teaspoon sesame oil

Freshly ground pepper to taste

Shake all ingredients in a covered jar or whisk thoroughly in a small bowl.

Makes 1 cup.

Anchovy Dressing

3 anchovy fillets, chopped and mashed
2 tablespoons wine vinegar
1 teaspoon Dijon-style mustard
1/4 teaspoon freshly ground pepper
1/3 cup olive oil

*I*n a small bowl mix together the anchovies, vinegar, mustard and pepper. Add the oil and mix thoroughly. Taste for seasoning.

*M*akes about 1/2 cup.

Sauce Verte

_____

_____

_____

1 cup mayonnaise

1/2 cup chopped spinach

1/2 cup chopped parsley

1/2 cup chopped watercress

1 tablespoon snipped fresh chives, or
1 teaspoon dried

1 tablespoon snipped fresh dill, or
1 teaspoon dried

2 teaspoons dried tarragon leaves

1 tablespoon lemon juice

Dash of salt

Combine all ingredients in blender or food processor and blend until smooth. Turn into a small bowl, cover and refrigerate.

Makes 1-1/4 cups.

Herb Sauce

1 bunch watercress
1 large bunch parsley
6 green onions
1 tablespoon Dijon-style mustard
1 teaspoon salt
Freshly ground black pepper, to taste
3/4 cup olive oil

Wash and shake dry watercress and parsley. Discard coarse stems of both. Wash and trim green onions, cut into 1 inch pieces. In the bowl of a food processor mince the parsley. Add the watercress and mince and then add the green onions and mince. Add the mustard, salt and black pepper and with the machine running, add the olive oil in a slow stream. The sauce will be thick but if it appears to be too thick to suit you, add up to 2 more tablespoons olive oil. Taste for seasonings.

Store in a glass or plastic container and cover tightly to prevent discoloration.

The sauce will keep under refrigeration for about 3 weeks and freezes well.

Makes about 1-1/2 cups.

Creamy Garlic Sauce

1/2 cup sour cream

1/4 cup mayonnaise

2 tablespoons light cream or milk

3 tablespoons tarragon or wine vinegar

2 tablespoons olive oil

1-1/2 teaspoons sugar

1 teaspoon salt

1/4 teaspoon freshly ground pepper

1 teaspoon crushed dry tarragon

4 cloves garlic, minced

*A*dd all the ingredients to the bowl of a food processor or a blender and blend until creamy.

*M*akes about 1 cup.

Parsley Pesto

4 cups parsley, coarse stems removed
1 cup walnut halves or pieces
1/2 cup Parmesan cheese
5 cloves garlic
1 teaspoon salt
1/2 teaspoon freshly ground black pepper
1 cup olive oil

In a food processor or blender process the parsley, nuts, cheese, garlic, salt, and pepper. Slowly add the oil and process until well blended. Taste for seasoning.

*M*akes about 1-1/2 cups. More than enough for 1 pound of pasta.

Spinach Pesto

1 10-ounce box frozen chopped spinach
1/2 cup chopped parsley
1/2 cup grated Parmesan cheese
1/4 cup pine nuts or walnut pieces
3 garlic cloves, minced
1 teaspoon salt
1/2 teaspoon freshly ground pepper
2/3 cup olive oil

*T*haw and squeeze as much water as possible out of the spinach.

*I*n a food processor or blender mix together the spinach, parsley, Parmesan cheese, nuts and seasonings. Blend thoroughly until smooth. With the motor running slowly add the olive oil. Do not continue mixing once the oil has been incorporated. Keeps about one week, refrigerated, and can be frozen.

*M*akes about 1-1/2 cups.

Spinach and Parsley Pesto

2 cups fresh spinach, tough stems
removed

1 cup fresh parsley, lower stems removed

1/2 cup good olive oil

1/2 cup freshly grated Parmesan cheese
or Romano cheese

1/4 cup pine nuts

3 large garlic cloves, halved

1 teaspoon salt

1/2 teaspoon freshly ground pepper

1/2 teaspoon oregano

Place all ingredients in blender or food processor and process until smooth.

Before using with pasta and/or vegetables, add 1 tablespoon of pasta cooking water to amount of pesto to be used. Store in glass container with thin film of oil on top, covered, in the refrigerator.

Makes about 1-1/4 cups.

Creamy Pesto Sauce

---

2 cups fresh basil leaves
2 hard-cooked eggs, quartered
1 cup oil, half olive and half salad
3 garlic cloves, halved
1 teaspoon salt
1/2 teaspoon freshly ground pepper
2 tablespoons basil or white wine vinegar
1/2 cup freshly grated Parmesan cheese

*P*lace all ingredients except oil in blender or food processor. Blend until coarsely chopped. Scrape down sides and blend again with oil until pureed.

*S*tore in a covered glass container in the refrigerator.

*M*akes about 1-3/4 cups.

Low-Calorie Creamy Dressing

1/4 cup mayonnaise, low cholesterol if possible

1/2 cup lowfat plain yogurt

1 tablespoon tarragon vinegar

1 teaspoon dry mustard

1/2 teaspoon paprika

1/2 teaspoon dill weed

1/4 teaspoon tarragon

1/8 teaspoon salt

*W*hisk all the ingredients together and refrigerate overnight or a few hours before using.

*M*akes about 3/4 cup.

Low-Calorie Mustard Vinaigrette

2 teaspoons Dijon mustard
2 tablespoons apple juice concentrate
2 tablespoons lemon juice
1/2 teaspoon basil
1/4 teaspoon oregano
1/4 teaspoon freshly ground pepper
1/8 teaspoon salt
1 pinch artificial sweetener

Shake all the ingredients together in a covered jar and leave at room temperature a couple of hours before using.

Makes about 1/2 cup.

Maxine Rapoport was born in West Allis, Wisconsin, and now lives in Washington, D.C. She has been creating, collecting and masterfully executing recipes for 20 years. She credits her mother with introducing her to the joys of cooking.

Nina Graybill, a Washingtonian, is a professional writer and editor as well as an accomplished cook.

For additional copies of

The Pasta Salad Book

Write:

Farragut Publishing Co.
810 18th Street N.W.
Washington, D.C. 20006

Please send me _____ copies of THE PASTA SALAD BOOK at $8.95 per copy
us a shipping charge of $.85 per copy:

ame_____

ddress_____

ity_____ State_____ Zip_____
Iake check or money order payable to FARRAGUT PUBLISHING CO.
nclosed is my check or money order for $_____.

For additional copies of

The Pasta Salad Book

Write:

Farragut Publishing Co.
810 18th Street N.W.
Washington, D.C. 20006

Please send me _____ copies of THE PASTA SALAD BOOK at $8.95 per copy
lus a shipping charge of $.85 per copy:

ame_____

ddress_____

ity_____ State_____ Zip_____
Iake check or money order payable to FARRAGUT PUBLISHING CO.
nclosed is my check or money order for $_____.